# The Voices Project
## 2011 & 2012:

## Tell It Like It Isn't &
## The One Sure Thing

*ACL* by Jasper Marlow
*Boot* by Joanna Erskine
*Brown Lips* by Nakkiah Lui
*Burnt* by Chris Summers
*Elissa Louisa Smith Loves William Cornelius Bennett Forever* by Sarah Hope
*First Light* by Vanessa Bates
*Fun in a Cup* by Tim Spencer
*Little Love* by Jessica Bellamy
*Mike* by Phil Spencer
*Pink Fireworks* by Finn O'Branagá.
*Principal* by Zoe Hogan
*That's What I Am Now* by Emrys Quin
*Twisted* by Georgia Symons
*Hunger* by Brooke Robinson
*The Circle of Life* by Alice Cooper
*The Last Post* by Sarah Gaul
*La Conversación* by Alexandra Macalister-Bills
*Stick* by Carolyn Burns
*Senseless* by Alex Cullen
*Ben Thomas, I Love You* by Alysha Herrmann
*Prince Willy* by Laura Hopkinson

CURRENCY PRESS
SYDNEY

australian
theatre for
young people

CURRENCY PLAYS

First published in 2012
by Currency Press Pty Ltd
PO Box 2287 Strawberry Hills NSW 2012
enquiries@currency.com.au
www.currency.com.au

National Library of Australia CIP data is available from the National Library of Australia Catalogue: http://catalogue.nla.gov.au

Typeset by Emma Vine and Paul O'Beirne for Currency Press.
Cover design by Emma Vine for Currency Press.
Printed by Hyde Park Press, Richmond SA.

This publication was supported by the Copyright Agency Limited Cultural Fund and the Graeme Wood Foundation

# Contents

# Introduction: Fraser Corfield

Welcome to *The Voices Project 2011 & 2012*, the first publication of scripts generated by young playwrights from Australian Theatre for Young People's Fresh Ink program. This important collection of monologues provides an opportunity for young Australian actors to present work tailored specifically for them by some of the country's leading young writers.

All Australian Theatre for Young People's programs are designed to support the next generation of story tellers. From writing ideas down, or having the confidence to perform or present them yourself, to the technical knowledge required to bring a performance to life through design, light and sound. The company believes that the best way to understand someone, to learn about something new, and to look at the world from another perspective, is to listen to their story. The Fresh Ink play writing program was started by Australian Theatre for Young People in 2008 thanks to the generous support of the Graeme Wood Foundation. Each year the company delivers a range of opportunities for young people to participate in workshops, masterclasses and forums on the craft of writing for performance. These programs bring young writers together with some of the country's most celebrated leaders to share ideas and experiences, to challenge preconceptions, and to find new opportunities. If you are interested in play writing I would encourage you to log on to the Australian Theatre for Young People website and get involved.

Australian Theatre for Young People celebrates 50 years of activity in 2013. The company has an extraordinary history in supporting young people realise their artistic potential. Young artists involved in the company's programs over the years have gone on to lead the performing arts in Australia. I've no doubt that if you pay close attention to the names of the writers in this collection you will find household names of the future.

Fraser Corfield
Artistic Director, Australian Theatre for Young People

# Foreword: Lachlan Philpott

As a drama teacher I used to try and lead students away from choosing solo performance for their Individual Performance. I'd make up stories about students corpsing in the exam. I'd throw reviews in their hands and tell them how much easier it was to criticise other peoples' work. I'd cut up felt and thrust scissors their way to encourage costume design... anything to make them see that performing was not the only way. Most of them were good performers. They could sustain a solo performance for more than six minutes in front of a couple of po-faced markers when it seemed their whole life depended on it. The actual performance wasn't the issue. It was finding the material to perform.

I close my eyes and travel back through time to that lesson when we all sat on the pea green carpet in the drama circle and I asked the class 'For those who have chosen performance, tell me what material you are considering for your IP'. Blankness. Nothing. The quest had begun.

And it is a quest. To begin work on your IP you need to find a monologue that hasn't been done to death but still works, a monologue which you can connect to as an actor which also ticks the markers' rubric. Teachers everywhere say 'Don't jump online and download material that is badly written or has no dramatic possibility'. And I always said 'since you are an Australian teenager try to avoid being an old Russian woman, a haughty southern belle or Rowan Atkinson'. Hands sweat, heads spin as the realisation dawns... selecting material for the IP is a confusing riddle.

This FRESH INK Voices Project was initiated to address the ongoing issue of sourcing material faced by the HSC Drama community. The project engaged emerging writers from The Fresh Ink program to create material for this purpose. The brief for each writer was to develop a new monologue that resonated as an authentic expression of a contemporary Australian teenage voice. When put together as a collection, the material would offer an exciting array of new stories and voices.

In 2010 the Fresh Ink writers visited drama classrooms in high schools in Sydney and spoke with students to get an understanding of the sort of material students would like to access and perform. It was an enthusiastic exchange which inspired a range of ideas and reinforced how important and necessary it was to create such material.

In developing the monologues each of the writers worked hard to ensure the voices were an authentic reflection of a contemporary teenage experience. They did this by testing and workshopping the material on the teenagers who would perform it. The writers also felt a strong desire to encourage the HSC Drama students to strive to connect to the same authenticity, challenging a commonly voiced assumption from students—which was that it was somehow not 'acting' if the role they chose to portray in their HSC was somebody their own age who was voicing an experience close to ones they have lived. I would suggest that this is closer to acting in the pure sense, which is about accessing and communicating truth.

The monologues in this collection are raw and provocative; truthful stories of young people making sense of complexities in their lives. They come from emerging writers from the Fresh Ink programs in 2010 and 2011. The first pod of monologues, born from the stimulus 'first love' were created in 2010 at The National Studio in Bundanon and performed in early 2011 in 'Tell It Like It Isn't'. It was a beautiful textured production which communicated how delicate we can be when it comes to expressing love. The response to this work in performance was extraordinarily positive. HSC students who saw the work were inspired because they were experiencing  performance which resonated with their own experience. There is nothing more exciting than watching a performance which has somebody in it who could be you.

After 'Tell It Like It Isn't' students and teachers demanded more. In 2011 monologues were developed. The second pod, dealing with issues of death and grief offer an interesting counter will premiere in at atyp in early 2012.

This is a collection of real, relevant and challenging seven minute monologues about seventeen year olds to be performed by seventeen year olds. Written by some of the most exciting emerging theatre voices in Australia they offer fresh insights into the world of the contemporary teenager. And if you happen to be on the IP quest, they are a rare treasure box of possibilities.

Lachlan Philpott
Fresh Ink Manager 2008-2011, Australian Theatre for
Young People

# Tell It Like It Isn't

## Cast List

| | |
|---|---|
| *ACL* | Felix Dupuy |
| *Boot* | Laura Hopkinson |
| *Brown Lips* | Rosie Connolly |
| *Burnt* | Joshua Forward |
| *Elissa Louisa Smith Loves William Cornelius Bennett Forever* | |
| | Julia Rorke |
| *First Light* | Kyle McLeavy |
| *Fun in a Cup* | Patrick Richards |
| *Little Love* | Danny Kim |
| *Mike* | Adam Marks |
| *Pink Fireworks* | Sophie Irvine |
| *Principal* | Gabrielle Nemeth-Taylor |
| | |
| Co-Director | Lachlan Philpott |
| Co-Director | Luke Kerridge |
| Costume Designer | Jasmine Christie |
| Production Manager | Liam Kennedy |
| Designer | Adrienn Lord |
| Sound Designer | Ekrem Mulayim |
| Lighting Designer | Chris Page |
| Stage Manager | Jonathan Ware |

# ACL

## Jasper Marlow

*Lights up slowly to reveal an agitated DAMIEN, late teens, wearing an Australian-rules jersey. He holds a Gatorade.*

**DAMIEN:**

What happened happened. Nothing I can do now. Y'know?

Sure. Be great if you could turn it back. But you can't. Simple as that. Anyway. This needs to be said.

Once. Then end of story. Ok? Good.

> *Pause.*

> *He opens the Gatorade and takes a swig calming down.*

Season starts today. First games at Nine [*checks watch*].

Y'into footy? I play second ruck. Have my whole life.

It's everything round here. If you don't play. You watch. And if you don't watch, you're not from round here... [*to audience*] no offence. Should've seen try-outs. Cold night, middle of the week and there's a crowd of people watching... Mad.

> *Pause.*

All started last year. Game before the semi when I buggered my knee. Tore the Cruciate Ligament... this bit. [*He points to his knee*] See the scar? Yeah. Jumped up for a catch, came down, whole thing just buckles. Gives way like it was made of sand. Like a million hot needles tearing into your leg. Spent 6 months on bikes, weights and gym mats getting back into top grade.

When try-outs finally came round. I was first at the pitch. Thought it would look good... plus I needed to stretch.

[*To knee*] Always on the back of your mind, that pain. Happened once, could happen again y'know?

> *He starts stretching his knee.*

Usual people were there. Matt, Ben…Greg. Normally we'd be joking. Talking about the weekend, girls, but something was up. Felt different. Tense. Greg pulls me aside me and says… 'Y'hear?' Hear what I say. 'Tiger juniors went bust.'

'So?'

'So their players are coming here and you're getting dropped.' I shrugged and said, 'We'll see.' [Laughing] Course I was shitting myself… but you can't show that. Not to them.

>    Pause.

When guys I didn't know started arriving everyone was silent. See. Footy changes at this age. It's not oranges at halftime anymore. It's for and againsts. Who's where on the table. Serious stuff.

Coach was setting up drills and everyone got in line ready to go.

## 2.

*Right before he blew the whistle, this kid runs onto the field still eating a sausage roll. Crumbs all over his jersey, shoelaces untied and a big smile on his face. Pathetic. We started warming up. My knee felt rusty. Sorta stiff. So I just went harder. Clenched my teeth, thought about the off-season, being stuck at home with Mum. Getting a job. Going back to school…*

>    Pause.

We got split up into our positions. Centre plays Centre. Back plays Back. Third Ruck plays Third Ruck. I stand and see who I'm up against. It's sausage roll. Easy. He pats me on the back and says, 'Good luck.'

>    *He re-enacts the play.*

We're off. Sausage Roll's not bad. Skillful. Flashy. But careless. Zig zags around. Handballs without looking. Game losing stuff. Suddenly Matt kicks the ball.

>    *He throws the Gatorade in the air like a ball.*

It's up. Spinning above us like a red torpedo. Me and sausage are shoving beneath it. Neck and neck. I can hear his studs on the ground, smell the tomato sauce on his breath. The ball starts falling. I jump to meet it. It's in my hands and I hit the ground. Hard. A sharp pain shoots through my knee and the ball flies out. I look up [*beat*] and see Sausage Roll kicking it between the posts.

>    *Pause.*

My fingers were shaking. It hurt to breathe. Hard saying it now, but tears were running down my face. That's how much it means to me… to the town.

I heard someone walk over and quickly wiped my face, pretended to stretch. It was Greg. He bent over, leaned right in my ear and whispered, 'Better luck next year, eh?'

>    *Pause.*

People hadn't left by the time I got up so I took backstreets. Walked down an alley and tried to think about something else. Anything else, but this voice in my head kept shouting, 'IT'S NOT FAIR. IT'S NOT FAIR.'

You do hard work. You get the reward. How life is. How it *should* be… but it's not. It's *fucking* not. So I started kicking garbage bins. Letter boxes… **Your** letter box. Sorry about that.

>    *Beat.*

And then I saw him. Ahead of me. Greg. On his mobile, smoking a Ciggy. Laughing. He didn't care about the team. Or hard-work. I couldn't control myself. It was like instinct, like in a game. I picked up a piece of wood lying in the gutter, gripped it so hard that splinters stuck in my hand and raised it above his head.

## 3.

*He uses the Gatorade as a plank.*

I took a breath and slammed it down hard. BAM. He fell to the ground. Phone smashed everywhere. Let out this little whimper and started to grab my leg. BAM. Hit him again. His nails dug into my shin. Just made me madder. BAM. Then he looked at me. Right into my eyes and we just stared at each other. He knew. Then, as if he accepted it… just let go. BAM. His head began to soften. BAM. BAM. Every hit got easier. Blood starts pouring out the gash. His hair was thick and black.

Then he was still. Didn't move. I dropped the plank and that's when *you* came out.

Must've been a shock. Especially being new in the area. But you have to understand something. We got a chance at the flag this year. Town does [*menacingly*]. Want to fit in, right? Part of the community? Then mind your own. Besides. You got kids. A boy? Yeah. Saw him at school once. I could give him lessons. Teach him about the game.

 *Pause.*

Anyway. Greg'll be fine. Coach sends round a tin at training. A gold Coin donation. Even says he might wake up one day, but I got his spot, so it's in good hands.

 *He takes a swig of the Gatorade.*

Knee's good now. Feels Strong. Can't wait to get out there. Join the boys. Might have to watch Sausage Roll though. Make sure he's committed. Anyway. Don't worry. Greg'll be fine… Greg'll be fine…

# Boot

## Joanna Erskine

*Dana sits in the school counsellor's office. She is determined not to speak. About 10 seconds pass.*

no

I don't need to

I

don't

want

to

sorry

   *She is silent again.*

I'm not the one to talk to

talk to her

I don't need to

I don't want to

no

   *Another silence.*

that's not true

that's not true did she say that

did she say that to you

I didn't

I

did

not

I

did

not

I

did

not

I

did

not

I

did

not

I

*Her words spew forth like a rupturing dam, as if without breath.*

here Julia gave me the keys they had an Air France key ring when did you go to France we go every year she said when actually I know her Mum just works in the head office—here take them—I'm not driving and we're not taking them

we are taking them

no Julia

we are taking them and you're driving bitch

and I know in that moment she knew she couldn't shouldn't drive but I wasn't gonna let her call me bitch so I said sorry bitch and I pushed her

the boys loved it they were off their faces yelling bitches please hurry the fuck up or pash or something and Julia yells you pash or something and someone said something about Dave being a homo and I can't remember much after that but then Katie turned up saying she couldn't get a cab either and so me Julia Katie Mike Dave Gavin Darren and Katie's sister Zoe all had to get into Julia's Mum's Peugeot

so that's eight of us and we all pile in and Zoe and Katie want to sit on the boys' laps and I said no fucking way we are taking the boys again I swear I said it so many times and then Julia says she can't get in trouble from the cops cos her Dad said he'd take her to Paris on his business trip so she said the boys had to lie down because there's been cops around and she doesn't want anyone not in a seatbelt so I say they're still not gonna be in a fucking seatbelt if they're lying on the floor and Julia says yeah but the cops can't see them and Julia's had like seven Stoli's so I shut up and I say fine I say fine fine fine and then I shut up I say nothing

so when the boys decide that the best thing to do the best idea anyone's had tonight is that they climb into Julia's Mum's Peugeot's boot

I shut up

because no one's listening to me anyway

Julia says if we get pulled over don't move don't fucking say a thing and then Mike closes the boot on Darren and Dave and Gavin and says have fun homos and we can hear them yell at him but it's muffled and once the engine's started we can't hear them anyway

so I'm in the front and Mike's in the back in the middle looking happy because he's got his arm around the sisters and they look pretty happy too sluts Julia gives me this look like she's thinking sluts too but Julia doesn't care cos her and Mike used to go out and she says he's a terrible kisser like injects saliva into your mouth it's not even worth it how good looking he is

so we drive

and it's late and there's not many cars on the road which is lucky because Julia goes over the lines and I have to grab the wheel and then I see what she's looking at in the backseat Mike injecting saliva into Katie's mouth and Zoe laughing and Julia says to me hold on and she turns the wheel so fast I hit her seat with my head and Zoe ends up with her head in Mike's crotch which he'd like except him and Katie whack their head against the window and crack their front teeth together so it's

what the fuck Julia and

fucking cow Julia and

fucking kill us why don't you Julia and

she laughs

she laughed

looking again at Mike and maybe she's

rethinking the kisses

because she is just staring at him
and I have to say
pull over
pull over Julia
and she ignores me
says
hey Mike want to know how fast I can go and he says
whatever
and Katie says just drop us home Julia
and Zoe says take the next left at that Shell
but instead
Julia floors it
and Zoe and Katie are yelling
stop it stop it
but Julia just laughs
again
and
goes faster
and faster
and faster
and faster
and starts to
swerve left
and right
and left
and right
into the
tree
  *Breathe, finally.*
and now everything is silent
and everyone has shut up

and for a long long long long time

no one moves and nothing

happens until I realise I'm ok

I remember being outside and saying phone phone does anyone
have their phone and I step over Gavin's legs and go around to the
other side of the car and I've just stepped over Gavin's legs without
the rest of Gavin and then I remember

the boys


in the boot

and again I'm saying

phone phone who has their phone

and then I called the police

> *Silence.*

that's it

that's all I remember

can I go

can I go

can I

no

that's not true

that's not true did she say that

did Julia say that to you

it's not true

I did


I

did

I

was the one

who called

and everything was silent

and everyone had shut up

I remember being outside and saying phone phone does anyone have
their phone and I step over Gavin's legs

and then I see you

> *Turns to Julia, who is sitting next to her in the counsellor's
> office.*

Julia

and you're looking at me

with that

face

I said to you phone phone

do you have your phone

and

you gave me your phone

and you opened the door

and

you

ran

you

just

ran

away

and I watched you

run

and when the police came

I told them you had gone

for help

and they traced your phone

and

because it came from your phone

they said *you* had made the call
and
that *you* went looking for help
and I
shut up
I just thought to myself
fine fine fine
I'll just shut up
and now you sit here
with your school captain sympathy badge
poor Julia poor poor Julia
I watch you accept hugs and flowers and have the news come to your house and be too depressed to go to the boys funerals and take your three months off school and watch your marks skyrocket and collect bravery awards because poor fucking Julia poor fucking brave Julia
when I'm the one who came back

> *Dana turns back to the counsellor.*

I'm not the one to talk to
talk to her
I don't need to
I don't want to
no

# Brown Lips

## Nakkiah Lui

Let's run away. Let's get out of this shithole. Let's go. We'll take off with dad's car. Come on sissy, let's go.
Let's go.

Now.

The sun glares at us. Des is staring straight ahead screaming along to some mixed C.D I'm pretty sure he was meant to make just for me. I close my eyes and imagine seeing the words come out of his lips. I open my eyes and all I can see are the small, see-through spheres of sweat on his brown skin above his lips.

I wanna lick them.

I wanna lick them right off. Right now.

My hair hits me in my face. The wind rushes through the windows. I let out a scream.
Those salty, beads of sweat. That brown skin.

The price tag hangs from the fake 'wayfarers' he swiped from the BP. He says to me, 'Check my back pocket,' and leans forward.

'Pull up my shirt.'
I lean in close against his bare back and I can feel my nipples get hard. I hope he doesn't notice. But I kind of do.
'Come on. In my pocket.'
There, red love heart shaped sunnies. I put them on and look up at him. He sticks out his tongue. I blow him a kiss.

I want to touch him. I want him to touch me. To know he is touching me. To know how it feels. How good it feels and I want him to feel it too.

We are together. On the run.

He leans back and says, 'Aren't you gonna ask?'

'What?'

'If dad knows?'

'Does Uncle Jim know?'

'Dad doesn't know.'

'Aunty Jan?'

'Nup.'

'Why?'

'Things get complicated.'

I don't know where he is taking me. I don't know where we are going. Things get complicated.

The bonnet is hot as I lay on it. I have on undies and a shirt. The metal is burning my bum.

There is a fly buzzing around me, occasionally landing on my forehead or my hand, and I just can't be fucked to swat it away.

In a way, even though he is here, the fly seems normal. I want it around. Because nothing seems real anymore. Me and Des.

Every night since I can remember I have dreamt of me and Des together. And now it's here. Nothing matters in the world but him and me getting out of this place.

The car rocks as he gets up and lays down next to me. He has no shirt on.

# Brown Lips

I realise it has been a long time since I have been with him with
no shirt on. When we were kids we used to have baths together.
Jumping around in the white bubbles.

I imagine that white froth against his tight, sweaty skin right now.
I swear I can see the bath bubbles on the short, dark hairs under his
belly button. I want to touch them. I want to run my hands over that
warm, slick skin. I want to grab at his sides and kiss his muscles. I
want to feel the soft, frothy bubbles on the black, sharp hairs.

The sun burns down on us so hard, I think it might be punishing me
for wanting him so bad. But it can't be, because his arms, his legs, his
entire body is touching mine and it feels so good. If it was wrong, it
wouldn't feel so right.

He starts to cry. Really cry. He grabs me and he sticks his face into
my neck. His tears run down onto my chest and our legs entwine.

I think I wind up enough courage to touch him. I must. Because Des
touches me. And he knows he's touching me.

Our dads are brothers. Des got his beautiful dark skin from his mum.
I got my fair skin from dad. My dad married fair. Des's dad married
dark.

INXS starts playing and the blue sky rushes past in a blur. Dream on
black boy, dream on white girl.

Des goes, 'Wanna go faster?'

I wanna go faster. I want to go so fast. I want to drive out of my
world and into his. I turn up the volume and Des plants his foot on
the accelerator. Inside of me the music gets louder and the pressure
from the speed builds up so fast I feel like I'm going to explode.

Faster, I scream. Faster! Faster!

The sirens are behind us.

Being in a fast car like this feels like something in my tummy is turning over. Like I've looked at porn.

Des pulls a strawberry lollipop he nicked from the BP out of his mouth and pushes the car to over 200. He sticks his finger up at the coppers. I suck on the lollipop and realise this is the best time in my life.

I'm dirty. And it's wrong. And if we had babies they would be retarded. But I feel free. We are flying.

The car is going faster than speeding light and no-one is gonna catch us.

The sirens appear in front. Speeding towards us.

He's yelling, 'Fuck, I thought we lost em. Fucking gubs.'

Des grabs my hand and looks at me. We are hurtling through this world together. The sirens are blaring and everything outside of the windows looks like a blur. I take off my heart shaped sunnies and I lean over and lick those beads of sweat from those brown lips and Des holds my hand tighter. His long brown fingers with big knuckles are squeezing my hands so tight as they tear us out of the car. Tearing us apart.

I scream, 'Des. Des.'

They throw me on the ground. I think someone kicks me in the side. They put cuffs around my wrists and pull my arms back so much, my tits bleed from being grated against the road. I don't cry because it hurts. I cry because I can hear him screaming. They are, were, hurting him.

I manage to look up from the ground as a foot is dug into my back. In the corner of my eyes I can see him being dragged into the back of a cop car. I could see the tiny, drops of blood glisten above his lip on that smooth brown skin.

I knew that things were never going to be the same.

Des, what would've happened if we never got caught? If we drove right out of Dubbo and we never got caught?

# Burnt

## Chris Summers

I'm in love with a monster.

We stand there, midnight, his waxy wings stretched out, held together by a spider-web of bones.

Flames pour out of his mouth, scorching cars and climbing walls.

Devlin.

Half Greek myth, half character out of *Twilight*.

He wipes his mouth on his sleeve.

     - I burn for you

First time.

Out the front of a club.

We watch each-other through traffic. His curly fringe red and blue under neon.

I fumble through my pocket to look like I'm not looking at him, but he sees so quick and suddenly—so fast—we thrust.

Trip.

Fall onto the pavement, panting and pants down.

Used condom in my hand.

My virginity gone.

We go out for coffee.

'What kind of a monster are you?'

     - A scary one.

'Are your parents monsters too?'

     - Are yours?

We fuck for millennia.

Skip school.

Mum calls him 'The Devil'.

I text Cassie.

- Are you serious? What does he look like? How old is he? What's his name? Are you going to take him to the formal? Wait. Wait. You're a *poofter*?

We burn.

We run through alleys and shopfronts, setting things ablaze, smashed glass and singed paper billowing behind.

We tear down buildings, bend lampposts and melt ATMs like birthday candles.

We terrorise the town cause there is nothing scarier than us.

And when we're dirty and tired, we sleep.

Me wrapped inside his wing.

In a cubicle, or a rusted car wreck, waiting for the morning sun.

'I want to know more about you'

- Nothing more to know.

Then I know him all.

Cassie tries on her dress.

- I got a big arse and I want people to see it. Especially now you aren't taking me. Single girl at the formal. Fucking tragic.

I can't stop seeing fire.

We giggle and drink tequila.
And we dance.

Thick flames.

Fast.

Quick.

But Cassie stops.

Lunges forward.

- Don't want to kiss me?

All this time.

Must be a poofter.

And then she makes me leave.

*Pause.*

'What do monsters do?'

    - You ask a lot of questions.

'I want to know more.'

He takes my hand and sends a firestorm of city smog and cinders into the sky.

We are destructive.

Wild, fiery, we are free.

And I'm only these things when I'm with him.

I notice by his shoulder a tattered patch of wing.

'Did someone do that to you?'

He watches me wait for him to answer and I feel something sink inside.

Something leaves for good.

Suddenly.

Footsteps.

A scream.

Two people down the street.

They stare.

Start running.

And Devlin swoops.

He swings into the air.

I run behind him as they run ahead.

We chase.

They scream.

Louder and higher.

More desperate, more alive.

And we follow.

We stalk.

Soar.

More.

Faster.

And more.

Trapped against a laneway wall.

> *Pause.*

'We can take their money. Let's go.'

Two tourists.

> - Ke pà de guàiwù!

They drop everything, hide behind their hands.

'Let's go.'

> - Yuan lí ke pà de guàiwù!

Devlin turns to me.

> - This is what monsters do.

Fire rolls.

Flames thick.

Fast.

Quick.

The wind blows away two bodies.

A sign above us reads: 'DEAD END'.

> *Silence.*

And then a service station somewhere.

We silently do what I now know is sex.

'Do you like my body?'

Loudly, he snores.

Something else I never knew he'd done before.

> *Pause.*

I wait for him.

Overlooking the harbour.

Waves, boats rocking.

Drunk teachers and seaborne spew.

Cassie's arse looks huge in the dress but she won't look at me.

Devlin arrives in a suit that fits like skin.

Everyone sees us.

Cassie disappears.

After seventeen years, for one second I'm noticed, and then everyone forgets.

- There's something I need to show you.

It all stops.

The music.

The couple in the corner mid-pash.

A still-frame formal.

He takes off his jacket and like a fleshy umbrella releases his wings.

We jump off the balcony and fly, blurring, the sky and the stars curbed.

Burnt seconds and smashed minutes trail off his wings like comet tails.

He shows me the town where he grew up and the farmer who gave him his first kiss.

He takes me to the river bed where he swam through summer til his bones broke.

He lets me listen to parents fighting, thrown punches in playgrounds and wet lips.

Bashings, crushed wings and blood.

We fly so fast and then we arrive next to a billion stars.

He puts his arm on my shoulder and mine around his waist.
We rock forwards, back, forwards, back.

- Monsters make people hurt.

Monsters don't fall in love.

You can't ever know a monster.

But I'll always remember.

I burnt for you.

Gravity lunges.

My body plunges.

Still-frame at the formal.

Except everyone else is moving again, but me.
The longest two nights pass.

# Burnt

Cassie calls.

    - Come on homo. We're going out.

'Am I a bad person?'

    - You're an arsehole, a wanker, a douchebag, a dickhead, a selfish shit-for-brains stinkface scrotum-sucker dirty slut and I love you.

My hair doesn't look right.

My eyes are red.

A mess of mega proportion.

In the shower, I notice my finger is burnt with a jagged squiggle.

Devlin had shown me an orange speck and said:

    - That's Mars.

    Pure fire.

    Don't touch it.

The burn grows black.

It spreads up my arm.

A branch.

Like a brand new limb.

    *Pause.*

    I wait at the bus stop.

    A little girl points at me.

        - Look at him, Daddy.

He's a monster.

    Gravity lunges.

    My body plunges.

    But still.

    I stand still.

    I whisper:

'There's no such thing as monsters.

    Just people who are burnt.'

# Elissa Louisa Smith Loves William Cornelius Bennett Forever

## Sarah Hope

**ELISSA:**

What mum?

*Pause.*

I'm in my room.

*Pause.*

I'm busy!

*Pause.*

No! Tell Tim to do it.

*Pause.*

I said, I'm busy!

*To audience.*

God. That woman. She never lets up. She's got no idea what goes on in my life, just nags, nags, nags. Yesterday, I get home from school and my brother has eaten all the apples. Meanwhile I'm starving, my tummy's been aching all day. I tell mum but she doesn't care. 'Eat a biscuit,' she says. A Biscuit? I don't think so. Honestly, the woman knows nothing about teenage obesity. It's amazing what parents don't know these days. So I nick Tim's favourite jersey and shove it down the toilet.

*Elissa picks up the rose and looks at it.*

There's this guy on Tim's footy team right? His name's William Cornelius Bennett, but we call him Bill. He's the sexiest dude ever. He has the lushest blue eyes, broad shoulders, big hands and dark kinda curly hair that he brushes out of his face all the time. I'd give anything to touch his perfect face and chiselled body. Oh. My. God. And did I mention he's got a voice that just kills me every time he speaks? It's all deep like,

'Hey Elissa, move your shit off my desk.'

*Elissa swoons.*

What a honey.

Jane, my B.F, once caught him naked after swimming. I was so jealous I didn't talk to her for a week. And I'm still kinda dirty. But don't tell her that.

I found it before class this morning. I get to my locker to take my books out and there it is, a long stemmed pewter rose. Under the rose is this note [*reads note*]

'Like my love for you this rose will never die, signed B.'

*She sighs.*

Bill loves me. That's why he was avoiding me at Eva's party on Saturday night. And it totally explains why he's always brushing past me in the tuckshop line. His firm pecks rubbing against my uniform, 'Yeah make way, eh?'

When Jane read the note she goes, 'O.M.G he like totes thinks you're awesome. I'll bet he asks you to the footy dinner.'

So I've been working on this poem for him.

### My Love is for Bill

When you look at me during break times at school

My heart skips a beat and I feel like a jewel.

You have saved me from a wicked fate

Of being trapped in a tower and never getting a date.

Of all the people in the world I love you the most

I can't wait for us to live together and eat vegemite on toast.

Happily ever after we shall someday be

When you hold my hand it's our love that they will see.

It needs work but you get the idea. I'm gonna present it to him after school tomorrow.

My first boyfriend! Oh Bill, how I love thee.

*Elissa exits and re-enters the following afternoon after school.*

William Cornelius Bennett is a total wanker. The guy walks around all day like he's top shit. Like he owns the school or something. Loser. Made my life a disaster just by existing.

So I arrive at school late this morning because it took me ages to do my hair. It does this thing where the bottom springs out and makes me look like I've been electrocuted or something. Mum reckons it would be easier if I just tied it back, but what would she know?

Anyways, I get to school and open my locker and this is waiting for me

> *She pulls out another note and reads.*

> 'Dear E, would you like to go out with me? Circle yes or no. B. x.o.x.o.'

[*Imagining how she felt*]. Oh William, your eyes sparkle with love. Keep me close, our hearts beating as one [*she taps her heart*] boom - boom, boom - boom. This moment should last forever. Kiss me my darling, kiss me like you've never kissed before!

> *She remembers the audience.*

I race straight over to the footy sheds where I know the boys will be training.

There he is, Bill, with his muscular quads warming up on the field. My heart is flying outta my chest. 'Wait,' I yell, sprinting in front of the team.

'Bill my darling, yes, yes, yes!'

Bill stops dead in his tracks.

'You beckoned me and so I came. Oh Bill, I've loved you for so long!'

[*In Bill's voice*] 'What the fuck?'

Bill goes 'Crazy bitch, as if' and just keeps going while the rest of the jerky jocks laugh at me and practically push me over as they run past.

Tim's the last to shove me and goes, 'Classic sis, you're so gullible sometimes.'

'What?' I scream in his face. 'You planted that stuff in my locker? You?'

'Yeah well, serves ya right for shoving a bloke's shirt down the dunny.'

[*Yelling at Tim*] 'Douchbag!'

Jane rushes over to rescue me. 'Those boys are idiots,' she reckons. 'And anyway, you're way too smart to be a footballer's girlfriend.'

She's totally right. I was a fool to think it would work between me and Bill. I mean he's pretty gross really.

But there is one thing I am sure of, Timothy Cedric Smith is gonna get it big time.

# First Light

## Vanessa Bates

*A young man, 17, uncomfortably dressed in a suit, stands, looking up at a window.*

*He throws a pebble up, sound of it hitting the glass.*
*A light shines down on him and he turns away.*

Sorry, that's, that's a bit bright, can you just…

> *The light dims a little. Pause. He is nervous, not used to announcing his thoughts like this.*

Hi.

Yeah I know what time it is.

Nearly dawn. First light. My favourite time of day.

> *Pause.*

There's a couple of things I needed to say.

To you.

So… the first thing was… I wanted to… to ask you… if you wanted to go with me… to the formal.

> *Beat.*

The one that was on two nights ago, yeah.

You're right. That *is*… shit. I didn't have the guts to ask you before.

But I wanted to show you… I did get a suit.

Just in case, you decided to ask *me*.

> *Lights abruptly turn off.*

Hey no! Please. I'm sorry ok? I'm sorry.

It's been a really intense day. You probably heard.

> *Light comes back on again.*

Thanks.

> *Pause. He launches in.*

Thursday night. Talking at work. That's how it starts.

Three of us. Me, Mike and Simmo.

Simmo's on about rockfishing.

For tuna.

Blue fin. Big shiny smart bastard of a fish.

Catch one, off land, you never forget.

Simmo's saying *Friday* and I'm saying nothing. Night of the formal.

Then Mike reckons he wants to come too.

Wants to try fishing off the rocks. Just once.

Simmo says it's all up to me.

Told him ages ago I might be taking you to the school formal.

Didn't tell him I was so pissweak I didn't have the nerve to ask. You and me.

What makes me think *you'd* be interested right? We barely speak at school, sit next to each other, in English, that's all. Hopeless.

So I say: *Let's catch some tuna.*

> *Pause.*

Night of the formal. I'm checking the gear. Lines, reels.

Pick Simmo and Mike up, 3.30 in the morning.

Gotta get to the spot before first light.

Walk through the bush

In the dark, for an hour

I can see these huge spiders, shining,

Strung out across the track.

Get to the spot.

Climb up the rocks, climb right out, ledge kind of thing, got a drop in front of you, two storeys down to black water.

I have a kitkat for breakfast, bottle of coke.

Simmo was told by a doctor to watch his weight so he has a cigarette.

Mike says he'll get a pie from the shop when it opens and Simmo goes :

*What pie? What shop?*

*You can't even get a mobile signal out here mate!*

Set up our stuff. Babypool for baitfish, balloons, rods, lines.

Watch the sun start to rise over the ocean.

First light. Everything bright

Shining like gold.

Feel you can do anything.

Say anything.

In that one moment.

I blow up a balloon.

See when you go to catch the tuna you put the baitfish on the hook

attach the balloon to the line—chuck it out

You watch the balloon, you know what's going on…

if the tuna's taking off with the baitfish…

if it's time to start reeling him in…

That's when I hear…

…hear Simmo scream

*FUCKING WAAAVE*

Look up.

Huge wave roaring towards us.

It's… a truck. It's a train. It's a massive friggin' building about to fall on top of us.

*GET DOWN!*

Drop.

Use my hands, my nails.

Grip on to the rocks. Hard as I can.

And just as this huge freak wave, wall of black water and fear, curls high above us…

I think… of you.

I want my last thought to be… of you.

Your hair, smell of your skin…

The way just being beside you,

not even touching,

It's like gold.

Feel it hit. Feel the smash.

Hear the crash.

Tears me back.

Skin ripped from my fingers.

Gut wrenching, chest crushing.

The terror.

Then it's gone.

I'm stinging. Aching. Alive.

I look up, see Simmo. *Where's Mike?*

*Where's Mike?!*

Then I hear him.

Two storeys below, in the ocean. The terror.

*Help me. Help me!*

Oh shit.

*Help me!*

I'm shouting: *keep away from the rocks, swim out mate. Swim out.*

*Help me!*

We look but everything's washed away.

Just a bucket, with a rope tied to the handle. And a lid.

So we throw that to him, he links his arm through the handle

hangs there in the water.

Never seen someone look so tiny. Helpless.

I take off, over the rocks, still got my phone, try and run up hill,

fast as I can, fast as I can.

ringing triple O, praying for a signal.

[*beat*] And I get it.

> *Pause. He composes himself. Calms.*

You probably saw the rest on the news today.

Jetski

Rescue.

Police

Ambos.

One billion tv cameras.

    *Pause.*

Mike's gonna be alright. Simmo's bought a lotto ticket.

And me?

    *Subtly, light starting to change as dawn approaches.*

I've been sitting here. Under your window. All night. Waiting for this.

First light.

When I feel I can do anything.

Say anything.

I want to say this:

    *Light suffusing the stage, gold. He straightens, breathes deep.*

Without you

there's no more fish in the sea, and I love you.

no more salt in the water, and I love you.

no more gold in the sky

and I love you.

And love you.

And love you.

    *Light intensifies and fades.*

# Fun in a Cup

## Tim Spencer

*ALEC sits on deckchair with a blue cocktail in a martini glass overflowing with brightly coloured decorations on the table beside him. He has braces, wears glasses, a singlet, board shorts and thongs. Between nine and ten o'clock in the morning. Growing heat.*

## ALEC:

You can see them all over this place. The heroes. The guys looking for attention and those who are so desperate to give it to them. I see them walking around the pool on the fifth deck. I see them with their fingers splayed out. I see them with their flimsy girlfriends in tow. A whole parade of nearly there, almost time and shoulda tried harder. That's the problem. A whole fucking boat full of trying too hard. You can smell it. There's a certain flavour of lynx effect for it. It sticks on the back of your throat and you keep coughing but it doesn't come. Like a piece of skin has come loose and is falling around in your air.

We got off on this island yesterday and Jake and I were walking around with Emily and Dean and we went to this beach and we just swam. I got out of the water and Jake was sitting there with my disposable camera and he said he took a picture of me. Me in the Pacific Ocean. I want to see the picture, that's the first thing I'm going to do when I get off this thing. I'm going to go to Kmart and get them to develop it. I'll go to Intencity for the half hour and after a few games of Time Crisis I'll go back and see what the photo Jake took of me looks like. If I look different in his eyes. If there is an answer or an equals sign between the way my best friend sees me and how I see myself.

It's been a big night. The last night of booze and naked swimming in the pool and Hawaiian shirts and cocktail umbrellas. I turned eighteen on this floating joke and nobody seemed to notice. The whole world kept spinning. There was an ice sculpture at dinner tonight. It was spectacular. A cornucopia of animals and food with a swan on top. A cornucopia is a horn like thing that is filled with food and animals and stuff. I don't know where it comes from. It's probably Greek or something like that.

This is hellish. There is nothing to say to these people. Seven days of saying and hearing things that I expect. Not a single new thing between us. A whole pile of why are you talking about this? Does it make you feel better when you talk about things that have no relevance to anything anyone has just said? Is there some plan behind it? Are you deliberately being dim? How's the weather, look at all this water, don't you look nice, what time is dinner, have you seen Jake, can I borrow your sunscreen, can I have a lobotomy please? Just get an ice pick and make your incision here. Don't worry about the mess, we'll do it on the top deck and the viscera will be washed away by the salt and seagulls.

I hate seagulls. In England they sound like seagulls are supposed to sound like. Here they just sound like singing cunts.

I've been watching Jake sleep. You get to know a lot about someone when you sleep in a two by four cabin with them for a week. He has a mole that looks like a cocoa pop on the small of his back. He talks in his sleep. He plucks his eyebrows. He spends ages in the shower. He reads MAD magazines on the toilet. He isn't circumcised.

Oh, the sun is coming out. You can see the city over there, and there's the Harbour Bridge. What a beautiful slut of a city. Nothing like it in all the world.

You know when you just have to say something. If you say it right things will fall into place. You get it right. You win. It's like that. I have this one chance.

    *Pause.*

We can all see the city. We've only got a few hours left on here. No one really explained this to me. A cruise. It's just a lot of sitting around and drinking and then a lot of standing around and drinking, then you get off and go to a beach and drink. The activities are there just to distract you from the fact that you've been drinking all day and you don't like anyone around you.

If I don't say it right I will never get another chance. I don't know what I want to say. I feel sorry for Jake. I pity him. I do. I look at his arms and legs and him in his pink board shorts and his monkey hands and I know that we are different people. We ordered an ice cream together in Cronulla one day when we were kids. He got chocolate and I got something exotic like boysenberry. We walked down the street together and he said to me, 'You're not going to be here forever.'

So this is it. Right back where we started from, a disappearing act from our city, our country, our parents. A shallow little Petri dish floating out through the Pacific Ocean. An ingenious experiment set up by the good scientists at P&O and Harvey World Travel. A grand scheme to separate the weak from the discontent, the horny from the merely pissed off. Fun in a cup. Fun in a fucking cup and garnish of paper umbrellas made in China.

Last night we went to this game on the big stage. It was after the rat eaten five minute rendition of musical numbers through the ages by actors who can't hack it on the mainland. There was this game on. Perfect Match. There were three chairs and one chair onstage. This dope with sequined purple lapels was asking for people to play. I fell into my gin and tonic to avoid him. I was just swimming around, hanging onto the ice, chilling out with the penguins. Then Jake pushes me onstage. The bastard pushes me onstage, he grabs me by the shoulder and yells my name and the whole place hears and there is green in his teeth from the bolognaise and everyone starts clapping and I know that he thinks I'm desperate, that I want to have sex because he's had and it was fucking awesome.

And here it is. Perfect Match. The thinly veiled attempt by P&O to get mingers and redheads copulating. Purple sequins asks questions. I answer. The cripple and pizza face next to me follow. The girl chooses me. She chooses me because I say things like, 'Amelie', 'Staffordshire terrier', 'Mauve' and 'A night in with a dvd'. She chooses me and we have to stand at the front of the stage and her blindfold comes off and she's terrifying looking and I'm red faced and smiling with the metal train tracks circling my face and I can see him. The son of a bitch in the back row with his arm around Emily laughing and drinking a cup of cider. I see him laughing and he puts the cup down then claps, there is a red and green disco light near his head and the right side of his face is green and the left side is red. And he's laughing. The girl next to me looks at me, is disappointed, grabs the coffee vouchers and falls offstage. I'm the main event and these people don't even know my name. They have no idea who I am.

This cruise is a round trip. The Treasures of the Pacific. We got on in Sydney and we return to Sydney. The same place seven days later. The same place, but I'm seven days older with a tan and a wood carving from Noumea that I'll smuggle past customs in a sock. And I can buy my own drinks. I come back as an adult. I have no idea what Jake comes back as.

# Little Love

## Jessica Bellamy

*Adam touches his eyes. He covers them. He moves a finger to his throat and touches the middle of his throat.*

**ADAM:**

Bat Eyes Barrett.

The blind girl. Ok, visually impaired. Visually impaired girl we call Bat Eyes Barrett. Her name's Jenny Barrett, but the joke's not as good when you say Bat Eyes Jenny. Doesn't alliterate the way we have to when we write poems in school.

Alliteration, metaphor, simile. Ticking the boxes.

Bat Eyes is a loser. Massively. Cares about work only, nothing else. We love to talk about her. Bat Eyes No Friends—half blind, half not. Her Dad wants her to go to a special kids' school, the bat eyes class. One of those schools way out of town. The ones you avoid. That sad feeling.

I look at her sometimes, but she won't look at me. Well, she can't.

Bat Eyes goes crazy over poems. Not the ones we have to write in class, the box-ticking ones, but the magic ones printed in books. The ones where it's hard to find where the alliteration is. Where it's woven in.

Delicate. But still there.

Bat Eyes learns the magic poems, the delicate ones, by heart. You walk out of class at lunch and she stays right at her desk, listening to the poems on tape. Line after line to herself, over and over, burning them in.

I walk past her, and there's one line she's saying to herself, '*Take down this book, and slowly read, and dream of the soft look your eyes had once, and of their shadows deep*'. And the words are welling around her eyes. Little wet ones.

I stop walking. Surprised. Didn't know tears could come out of bat eyes, especially Bat Eyes No Friends. And I stand there and watch and try to see what's happening to her eyes, what is moving around inside them and under them to make them cry like that.

And then I do something stupid. She hears me come up there and stand in front of her. She says my name. 'Adam'. She knows it's me, I don't know how, because I don't limp or stomp or anything.

She knows my footsteps. And she knows my name, which I wasn't sure she did 'til now. She knows it's me there, and she says, 'Sorry Adam. It's just so fucking beautiful'.

And then I say it. The stupid thing.

'How would you know what's beautiful? You can't even see.'

> *Long beat. He touches his eyes.*

Knows my name. Knows my footsteps. And that's what I've got.

It freezes. My words hang there. Bat Eyes lifts her hand, and finds them between us. Finds my mouth that shot them out. Finds my cheek, and goes, *smack*.

> *He touches his cheek.*

She smacks, and she looks at me and her bat eyes flash. Alive. She lifts her hand off my face and blinks. Wet words everywhere now, running down her cheeks. And those bat eyes flashing. Stars.

I don't know what she's going to do.

> *Adam gets his index finger and very slowly places it on his forehead. He runs his finger from his forehead down to the middle of his throat—Adam's Apple height.*

She stops there, finger on my throat. Pokes, strokes.

'*That's* where it's beautiful. Tastes and sounds and feels.'

And then that's it. Circles on my throat. Mouth dry. Stars in her eyes, finger on my skin. Bat Eyes.

She lets me follow her home, right into her room. It's a rainbow. Velvet cushions, silk bedspread, curtains made of organza. Flowers—crisp and fresh and sweet. Tinkly things and water sounds. A chugging fan. A leather desk. Things to touch and smell and hear—everywhere.

And I don't know where to start. What to touch. If I've imagined it all. And if I have, why am I here? Why did she invite me?

All that, swimming round, while I'm looking into her bat eyes. Waiting for them to come alive again. To do something. Anything.

   *Beat. He runs his fingers around the outline of his lips.*

I didn't think that was something you do to a boy. But she does it. She touches all around my lips, and then her bat eyes flash. They really properly flash and she says, 'Just once. Souvenir.'

   *Beat.*

And before I can think any more, she's pulling me on top of her. Kissing my dry mouth. Finding skin under clothes. Ready, both of us, to lose it together. The poem is moving under our skin, in our eyes—*'and bending down beside the glowing bars'*—words pulling us into each other. Their flash, their stars.

And then it's over. She rolls around and says, 'Thank you' to the wall and I don't know what to say. I reach out to turn her round, to see her bat eyes again, and she won't let me. There's a bloodstain on the bed and she finds it with a finger. Traces the edges. Probably gross to anyone else, but not to me.

'Little love,' she says.

And then I know.

No more Bat Eyes stuck at her desk. No burning words over lunchtime. We've had each other, and now we don't. Loved each other for a minute. But over now.

The stars won't come back like that. The words won't flash the same.

And I lie on my side, and look at the back of her head, and mouth the rest of the poem to myself. *'Murmur a little sadly how love fled, and paced upon the mountains overhead, and hid his face amid a crowd of stars.'*

And that's it. All of it.

Bat Eyes and me. Short and little. New stars. New poems.

But still, love.

# Mike

## Phil Spencer

*Late afternoon. A large shopping mall. Mike (17) stands next to a pram.*

**MIKE:**

This is Jordan. My son. Yeah. I'm his dad. I'm a dad… a proud dad. Cos he's awesome, he's amazing, he is ay. So little and squishy like a… like a… sock, all rolled up and bundled in there.

> *Slight pause.*

We're a little family. Me, Claire and Jordan. We don't live together or nothing but still counts. We're still a better family than my mum and dad. Wouldn't catch Claire and me fighting like that… name calling, smashing stuff. No fucking way… oh sorry, I gotta stop swearing. Gotta learn ay. What I mean is nope, you wouldn't catch us fighting.

> *Pause.*

We got a little baby boy, who has ten fingers, ten toes, even if two of them are still stuck together, and a healthy little heart. Proper family photo ay?

> *Pause.*

I know what you're thinking. I do. I can see it. You're thinking, 'They're young.' You're thinking, 'What a waste.' I know you think that, it's written all over your face. Well fuck… [*Under his breath*] Fuck you!

> *Pause.*

Claire was in labour for forty minutes. Yeah, forty minutes, that's less than an hour. Nurse said it was easy. Said it was because Claire was 'child bearing' age, or… or whatever. Said that at sixteen Mother Nature just… feels a bump… scoots to the hospital… pop… all over in a flash. I don't know what all the fuss is about.

> *Pause. Mike looks over at the pram.*

Little critter.

*Slight pause.*

Was weird at first. When I first found out about… Claire… you know being preggers and that. We'd only done it once, well once properly. Fucked up ay? I freaked out a bit. Cos I thought it'd be like, well thought it'd be… I dunno… real shit I suppose.

*Slight pause.*

Claire text me on the Thursday night, saying 'PLS CALL ME ASAP'. So… I did. She was kinda blank when she said it. No crying, or moaning, just, 'Hey Mike, we're going to have a baby.' Mad ay?

*Pause.*

Telling my rents was easy. I didn't really care what they thought.

*Pause.*

I was worried about telling the lads. Found out the Thursday night. Couldn't go to school Friday and didn't play Saturday. Just sat at home freaking. They're pretty cool about it now, the lads. Well, all of 'em except Dan. Dick. He's just pissed cos he fancies Claire and he ain't gonna get shit now, cos we're a family ay? Cos we're stuck together now, proper. Good stuck.

*Pause.*

Bought him a new T-shirt toady. Look. It says 'Fuck Off Pedo, I'm With Daddy'.

*Pause. Laughs.*

Claire will love it. Funny stuff like that works.

*Pause.*

He don't do that much yet, but he will. He'll grow up, proper, and be something. You know, like something he wants to be, like a footy player or a film maker and that. I'll send him to college, maybe the same one that I'm at now.

*Slight pause.*

Long way to go yet though.

*Beat.*

He cries. A lot. But that's normal ain't it? It's how you know they got brains and that cos they're telling you they don't like something.

*Beat.*

My mum says it's what I did when I was little.

*Beat.*

Claire can be annoying sometimes… says that he's dumb like her, says that he's wrong somewhere. There ain't nothing wrong, he's just little that's all.

*Beat.*

You just got to tell him, if he keeps crying… tell him, 'Look son, be good for daddy. Don't make a scene in the shops.' Got to look at him, treat him proper and say, 'Not in front of daddy's mates. Be a good boy Jordan.' You got to talk to him, cos he gets it, he docs. 'Mummy will be out soon… just… just… stop.'

*Pause.*

But sometimes it's harder ay. Like today. Hanging out with Tomo and Felix. Just chilling and that, Jordan too. No big deal. Claire just needed to go get stuff, girl stuff from the shops, so yeah we'll bring the little guy along to Red Rooster. No worries. It wasn't a big thing just… Jordan being… you know crying and that ay. But you got to keep your cool.

*Beat.*

We're sat down—Felix gets three burgers and sundae, fat fuck. Jordan starts up. 'Maybe he's hungry,' Tomo says and he tears a bit of burger bun and chucks it into the pram. He keeps shrieking. Keeps wailing. Keeps turning his little cheeks red. 'Give him the boob Mike, give him your boob,' Tomo laughs. Felix just drops his shoulders, 'He's really loud man.'

*Beat.*

I pick him up, his pudgy feet kicking. Screaming. Fucking keeps screaming. 'Come on Jordan, not now.' 'Let's get outta here,' Felix mumbles. Jordan getting worse and worse. Wriggling around like a worm. Whole place is looking over. And I know what I shout ay. He needs to understand don't he? Cos, I'm the dad. And he's not listening. He's ignoring me. Felix and Tomo start stuffing their burgers and getting up to leave. He keeps screeching.

'Stop it…now.'

And yeah I move him. A bit. I move him around to show him.

'Shhhh Jordan, be quiet.' He keeps crying. Keeps rolling around.

'Shhhhh.' I sort of shake him. A little. Just like.

'Shut-up, shut up.'

> *Beat.*

I hold his face next to mine. He won't listen.

'Shut up! Jordan! Just shut the fuck up!'

> *Long pause.*

Felix and Tomo were gone. Bolted. I look around and she's standing there. Stood there looking at me. Glaring at me, with dart eyes ay. She runs over pulls him out of my hands. Takes his head and kisses it. Bundles him up into her, turns her back and just walks off with him. Just leaves, no shouting or that. Just leaves me and the pram stood here.

> *Pause.*

I feel sick.

> *Beat.*

But she… she can… well, Claire can piss off anyway. Stupid bitch. If it weren't for Jordan I'd have ditched her ages ago.

> *Pause.*

I never hurt him. I didn't. I know… I know it was a bit heavy but I'm his dad he's got to listen. He's got to understand me as well.

# Pink Fireworks

## Finn O'Branagáin

She made me a ring in metalwork.

A squiggly thing, like silver seaweed.

'I made you a present.' She chirps and tosses it over.

You give rings to people you care about.

People you love.

No one ever made a ring for someone they didn't love.

Something wriggles and grows inside of me.

A tightening and warming of my belly.

All those 'girl nights' not quite being sure if she was playing with me.

Not knowing if lying on piles of clothes for hours is just what girls do when they are best friends.

Or holding hands. I don't know if she holds hands with her other girl friends.

But a ring…

Surely that is something?

You don't give rings to your best friends.

You give those half broken heart things, or those beaded wrist band things.

A ring that you make is for more.

Surely.

I look up at her face. She always looks like a magazine photo.

Her coloured braces things match her shoelaces this time.

'Thanks,' I breathe, and there are only her eyes. I smile like the ring is diamonds and we are in a pop song video on Channel V. Like that song about kissing girls wasn't just a gimmick and we can prove it.

It's one bit of wire, all squiggled around and welded. The ends are free, and a bit sharp. It's a bit big, but it fits on my thumb. I clasp my fingers around it and get a little scratch.

It's ok.

.......
.......

It's the end of the day, and a bunch of us are walking to the shopping centre. It's cold, so we are all kind of huddling together. We are walking close, our arms linked. I can feel her muscles and flesh under her uniform jacket. Her warmth. I try to make the most parts of my arm touch the most parts of her arm.

She lights up a cigarette and rubs her hands together. I wonder what that will taste like. If it will be woody or leafy or taste like it smells. If it will be different from kissing boys. Softer, or sexier. If girls spit tastes different. If a smaller mouth will make a difference. What kissing someone with braces will be like. And I'm not sure if I'm ready but I definitely will try to be.

She slips her hand down to mine. 'You're quiet, babe.'

I run my thumb along her thumb and squeeze. She lets go. There's always this kind of awkward moment when one person lets go anyway. It's this, 'Oh, yeah, it's fine' thing. It's like when you hug someone and they pull away while you're still squeezing.

::::
::::

It's my bus home. We look at each other while we decide if she'll come over. We've got assignments, so she's going to go to hers to finish.

We hug goodbye, and my heart goes like one of those stupid car stereo things. Our cheeks brush, and I wonder if we'll kiss a little bit. But we're at a shopping centre and it's a bit weird and she just kind of yells, 'Bye,' and walks off with the others.

My heart keeps pounding on the bus home.

The shopping centre isn't the best place for a first kiss anyway.

:::::
:::::

At lunch next day I rush to our table at recess to wait for her.

The other girls start to emerge from their classes.

We sit around, like usual, but now it feels like they are the extra ones, instead of me being the extra one. Like if we were off sick, the conversation wouldn't be so fun. Lunch would be boring.

Like we are the lights. Like Lisa and Bel just rolls off the tongue even better than best friends.

I smile at our secret.

Claire comes bouncing up, she's already spilled tomato sauce on her uniform. 'Did you give it to him?'

'No, I thought Bel would like it better.'

My breath stops.

Blood is pounding in my head. I am sure they can see what is happening. See my mistake. See what an idiot I am. Surely I am blushing set to catch fire.

'Chickenshit.'

They all laugh and I laugh that hollow laugh.

::::::
::::::

I keep the ring.

In my pencil case so I can see it in class when I start to forget.

A reminder not to be an idiot.

::::::
::::::

She asks me if I want to come over after school.

I nearly say, 'No' but…

We lie in her room with the cd player on, talking about people at school.

I get that kissing feeling rush up on me.

I think of her kissing Brandon and something falls in me.

But I still have hope.

Fuck it.

I have been hesitating for ages. I feel like everything I am doing is in strobe lights.

I kiss her.

We both breathe in quickly.

I feel her lips against my lips and for the split second I am terrified.

Will she push me away?

Will she be angry?

And then she will tell everyone at school that I'm a freak and a pervert and it won't be cool like the girls who do it at parties because they are drunk and boys are watching. It will be awful because it's real. Like Daniel making that little safety pin tattoo of Josie's initials on his arm is real. We laughed at him. They will laugh and I'll have to sit by myself and I will die.

But she doesn't.

Her lips move.

Soft.

Sexy.

Her lips open, and our tongues crash together like pink fireworks.

She is kissing me. It is perfect.

And then it's not.

And then she is pulling back.

'What are we doing?'

I can't talk.

I wait for her to yell at me.

She grins and giggles and hides under one of her t-shirts from the pile under us.

'Silly!'

And then she's just talking again.

Like nothing happened.

Like it's ok.

Like you can just kiss someone like that and have no consequences.

Like she does at parties.

::::::
::::::

I think about leaving the ring at her house.

At home I look at the ring. It is pretty crappily made. A ring shouldn't scratch you while you wear it. It's not even welded properly. She could have failed that prac. I would have failed her.

*She starts to unravel the ring. She pulls it all apart.*

# Principal

## Zoe Hogan

*A girl sitting on a chair.*
*She raises her hand.*

I'd just like to say something.

I'd like to say, I don't think it's fair. What you're about to do.

It's not like he killed anybody or anything. Not really.

It was an accident and what you're about to do to him isn't right.

> *She stands up.*

I know we're just kids and we don't have all that life experience and shit that you keep telling us about. Like when you trekked through Patagonia with a llama and painted a wall at a school or whatever.

But we do know some stuff, like what's right and what's wrong. And what's neither.

And because we're kids you probably don't think we can talk about big things. Because we don't know enough about them. Like love and sex and war and betrayal.

The things you put in capital letters.

But I do know.

I know betrayal is Mr. Quinn sleeping with Miss. Suarez even though his wife's preggers.

I know war is what goes on in the girl's toilets, every day after recess and lunch. Mints all round after.

I know sex is what keeps us going round behind the drama rooms, just because we wanna have a look under each other's uniforms. We want to know what everything feels like.

I know about love.

I know about love not because I love my dog or dolphins or because I have to say it to my dad over the phone since he moved.

I know what love is because I'm in love with the boy who's sitting in your office.

The one you're about to expel.

And yeah, you think I'm naïve and stupid for loving a boy at school. It's such a cliché isn't it? High school sweethearts. If you aren't one, you know one, or you were one, and if you're not one you want to be one.

I am one and it's not sweet. We're in love but we don't write each other letters and I don't think he's perfect and he doesn't think I am either.

That's how I know it's real.

I know he didn't mean to hurt him. You can't expect to employ a geriatric to mulch the school grounds and not have consequences.

That's what gets me. You expect your elders to shovel round bits of wood that have been treated to be just the right shade of 'burnished maple' that you picked in a landscaping catalogue? Shoveling round bits of mulch till he's ready to drop dead?

And when a boy on a bicycle comes round a corner—a blind corner—isn't there a clause in some huge OH&S manual somewhere about blind corners?—and clips the old man, the gardener, the shoveller of your rotten consciences, and because of that clip the old man's heart is shaken into a state of beating, beating, beating, as if he's a young man in the throes of first love again, and that heart beats so fast that it can't take it anymore and it stops, is it really the boy's fault?

And if the boy happened to be racing round the corner, backpack bulging with certain magazines found underneath his big brother's bed—certain magazines whose subject is always in fashion and resale value always intact—if he was rushing on his way to a meeting, a business meeting, to sell these magazines to earn some extra pocket money, which he may or may not have been intending to use to buy a certain girlfriend a certain bracelet she's wanted for a very long time, is that really so wrong?

    *Silence.*

Don't worry.

I don't expect you to answer.

Like when you ask us: what does this school stand for?

And what are our responsibilities?

And where do we see ourselves in the future?

And why do we highlighter our hair?

And why do we white out our nails?

And the worst one of all, my favourite—do you know what's it's like out there, in the real world?

>   *Pause.*

Intercom to the staff room: we're already there.

Tom's mum has cancer.

Shell drags her left leg around like it's not connected to her body.

Hanna can't make it through the day without crying.

Brendan was punched for kissing his boyfriend at the shops.

Greg is so afraid of not getting a band six he hasn't been to a party in three years.

And I'm in love with a boy who thinks soft porn is a business opportunity.

That boy is going to be my husband, and I'm sorry to bring it back to me, but the fact is I don't want to have the responsibility of supporting a family on my own because my husband was kicked out of school and went off the rails when he was 16.

>   *Pause.*

Everyone has to go sometime. He had a good life. He got free lunches from the tuckshop and perved on PE lessons. It's not so bad.

So, like, what I'm saying is… just have a heart.

I'm in love with him.

And I want him to finish his exams.

# The One Sure Thing

## Cast List

| | |
|---|---|
| *That's What I Am Now* | Patrick Richards |
| *Twisted* | Shaun Foley |
| *Hunger* | Rhys Keir |
| *The Circle of Life* | Alistair Mcintosh |
| *The Last Post* | Emma Khamis |
| *La Conversación* | Charlotte Hazzard |
| *Stick* | Emma Campbell |
| *Senseless* | Kate Campbell |
| *Ben Thomas, I Love You* | Julia Rorke |
| *Prince Willy* | Lucy Coleman |
| | |
| Director | Tanya Goldberg |
| Stage Manager | Asha Watson |
| Designer | David Fleischer |
| Sound Designer | Kingsley Reeve |
| Lighting Designer | Verity Hampson |
| Assistant Director | Liz Arday |

# That's What I Am Now

## Emrys Quin

*Enter JAZ, she is played by a man. She is an energetic 17 year old in a T-Shirt and jeans. She is sipping tea from a large mug.*

**JAZ:**

You never made being a woman easy, Granny. It was always God inspects, and God expects, and Goddwells in retrospect—by retrospect I always pictured God in flares—but you did give me a sense of duty, y'know?

> *JAZ begins walking slowly on the spot, the pace of her voice will match the pace of her movement.*

JAZ: Well that's what I am now; dutiful. I got a job—my first one. I'm always on a bicycle; backpack filled with pharmaceuticals. That's what I am now; pharmaceutical courier, been one for a while actually – Golly! We haven't seen each other in forever! Well they say on my employment review I'm smiley. That's me all over, I think: smiley—and dutiful.

> *JAZ sips her tea. She quickens her pace.*

JAZ: Today was a special delivery list, y'know? Three names; Graham, 82, Michaels, 81, and Greene, that's you Granny, 89. You're all spread across the city like entrails across a water biscuit—this is lovely tea—Graham answers the door himself, takes a breath and says, real arthritic and English like 'now what the fuck do you want, young lady?' while Michaels, just a little old fashioned, doesn't mince words when she answers the door.

'Are you seeing anyone, Jasmine?'

'Yes ma'am.'

'Surname?'

'Putnam, ma'am.'

'Is that Jewish?'

'No ma'am.'

'Very good, they've got noses like Satan's sphincter.'

> *JAZ sips her tea.*

JAZ: Wow. This tea—it's just honey and dandelions, y'know?!

> *JAZ is now jogging. She speaks in a hurry concurrent with her jog.*

JAZ: One more left after that, it's you. I take the high road, it's quicker—that's what I am now; smiley, dutiful and punctual. I speed a bit, through traffic too, but I'm at your street quicksmart, and up to your door. There's the doorbell; brief buzz and I'm inside, jumping up three flights of stairs and suddenly I'm in your doorway—in front of you, Granny, here, Granny.

> *JAZ slows to a walk and stops, she returns to a natural speaking pace.*

JAZ: You look at me a while, like you're not sure what to say. Standing there on your venetian rug, the expensive one—I smile, know it's down to me to make you feel comfortable, duty of a granddaughter: 'hey granny!' I say, 'surprise!' no response, but I keep on: I leap right in—tell you about my new job, how I'd finally got to deliver to you. Still nothing, so I ask you for a cup of tea—Fantastic tea—and you grumble before you're off into your tinny little kitchen. Fiddling with the kettle, but it boils real quickly. I let myself in. Close the door.

'I've been going to church' I say. 'Good' you say—the first thing you do say—

I know there's only three things you wanna talk about: men, children or Jesus.

'I'm seeing someone,' I say, you make this grunting noise, sort of non-committal hatred but that's okay, I'm smiley—

'Her name's Tanya.'

> *JAZ sips her tea.*

JAZ: You drop the jar of sugar—rather messy—spin around and look at me, cup of tea in your hand. I try ignore the rabid, burning, loathing glare you're giving me, just take the cup and say 'golly, thanks grandma!' but it's obvious you're mad, really mad, like lesbianism's worse than paganism and American television. This is just eye-melting phwwwooooaaa kind of tea.

*JAZ sips her tea.*

JAZ: I wanna talk to you about my first pap smear—I mean that's where I met Tanya. She was on the desk, y'know? And sure I'm only 17 but my job gets me free check-ups and I just sort of couldn't help myself: I get the lot—all the check-ups, I mean, even the real invasive ones, just to see what its like to be—a woman. She had real short red hair—not slight red, but great, fiery stuff, something out of Irish mythology, I walked up to her, sort of mesmerised, y'know? I couldn't stop myself, just asked

'What are you?'

and she grinned with these gorgeous yellow teeth, and said

'University dropout.'

Wasn't what I meant but I went along with it—I smiled back and said 'I'm an HSC student with religious and femininity issues,' and she just said 'cool,' and leaning closer, grabbed my wrist with this colossal grip, whispered 'wanna fuck?'

*JAZ sips her tea.*

JAZ: I left with her phone number and some test results—and golly while I tell you this you just get white as the Holy Ghost, Granny—I'm not sure what the scientific term is but the doctor told me I had 'deadbeat ovaries'—lazy reproductive system, y'know? That's what I am now: smiley, dutiful, punctual, lesbian, barren. Infertile. No great grandchildren kind of thing, and you just murmur, real spiteful like, 'you'll forever be a girl, lost to God and confused'.

And I say, 'golly, grandma, you know there's more to me than a uterus and a ring finger, right?' But you just step right up close and say 'I never want to see your sinner face again, you little whore'

—or something like that—

but that's okay, I'm smiley, and as you turn around, back toward the kitchen; I grab the copper crucifix you keep on the little table underneath the window—and I start to beat you to death with it. Cleave a chunk of skull, then your neck, work my way down real slowly—Golly! It's rather gorey business, soft wet crunch ringing in my ear as I wail hard and heavy into that bone between your breasts—keep on until there's not much bone left, until—until I stop, and eventually you do too—living I mean—and by that time your venetian rug is rather ruined.

> *Brief silence. JAZ sips her tea. She begins to walk on the spot again.*

JAZ: Then comes the adrenaline. Like a freight train through a window. Snap upright. Move over to the bag—my bag—get the kerosene. Clear container marked 'Experimental cough medicine'. Open it. Real methodical like. That's what I am now: smiley, dutiful, punctual, lesbian, barren, methodical. I unscrew the lid.

> *JAZ pours tea onto the floor as she describes dousing her granny's corpse with kerosene.*

JAZ: Pour it over your ankles, your stomach, your arms, your eyes. Pour it over wrists, lips, shoulders, hair, around your neck, your ears—ears that never really listened when I asked the stupid questions like

'what's my house gunna look like, granny?'

'you won't have a house, your husband will'.

> *JAZ empties her tea. She disposes of the mug. JAZ picks up her pace.*

JAZ: Container's empty. Fingers shaking like God's fist at the scientologists. Marry a guy, have his kids, keep his house—then you're a woman, yeah? Yeah? Heaven, hell. Man, woman. With us or against us. It's called a dualism! It's called extremism, and religious extremists are just souls on a swing-set that God isn't pushing! What if I can't love a man?! What if I can't keep his house?! What if I physically cannot have his kids?! Where does that leave me?! Can't toss the container here. That'd be silly—I'm not silly. I've wised up—that's what I am now, smiley, dutiful, punctual, lesbian, barren, methodical, seventeen and wised up. I mean the way I see it—God made us all with a purpose, if I can't give life, then I was made to take it away! My dualism!

> *JAZ goes for her matches in her back pocket. She picks up her pace.*

JAZ: Get the matches. Back pocket. Fingers are shaking—stop it, Jasmine. Need to move quick, people get suspicious when bodies start piling up. Bodies, yes Granny, bodies, plural—yours, and Michaels, and Graham—me and Tanya up til dawn pouring washing powder and arsenic into little capsules—fucking fiddly little things—few hours later I drop them off in regulation packets—it's like pigeon culling but with pensioners. Open up the packet, pull out one slender stick—modern medicine's a dualism, Progression by regression type of thing, that's what Tanya says, no social benefits for making concessions for the weak—that's you—sold your brains to the church for social security. Think because you've outlived happiness God owes you something! WELL THAT ISN'T ME! I'M SMILEY! I KNOW WHERE I FIT IN THE DEVINE JIGSAW PUZZLE! SEVEN BILLION PEOPLE ON THE PLANET AND GOD'S RUNNING OUT OF PATIENCE WITH THE ONES WHO REFUSE TO DIE! THAT'S WHAT I AM NOW; HIS WILL FUCKING DONE!

> *JAZ leaps to a halt, she points insidiously to her grandmother's corpse with the matchstick.*

JAZ: AM I A WOMAN NOW, GRANNY?!

> *Brief silence.*

JAZ: Granny?

# TWISTED

## Georgia Symons

*Michael is 17 and disheveled. He jumps down from atop a high fence into 'the valley'—an out-of-bounds area just beyond the school fence. Having landed, he motions for his friend TOM to join him.*

## MICHAEL:

Come on, dickhead. It's like two metres!

> *He waits. TOM hesitates.*

Fucken hell. Every time, man! Miss Jenna's not gonna miss you in class dude, it's like two weeks from holidays, no one's taking rolls.

Come on, Princess. Bend your knees, that's the way.

> *MICHAEL watches as TOM makes the jump.*

[*Sarcasm*] Flawless landing, bro, gold medal stuff.

> *Pause.*

Thanks. For coming.

> *Pause.*

Miss Jenna's a bitch anyway. She 'n' my mum go to town on me every single parent teacher night, it's fucked. Anyway you know I wouldn't make you jig just to come 'n' piss about in the valley, I just… I gotta tell you about last night.

So I go to Kayley's and we're hanging out in her room, and I'm ready. I've got the whole thing nailed. So she's chatting away about her new Maltese Poodle, and I tell her that Malta doesn't have Poodles, it's got, like, grapes and dead Italians, but she's called the thing Miffy and she doesn't care what fucken dog factory it came out of, and then I get distracted by a bit of her bra poking out of her top, so I let it slide.

So anyway we're talking and everything, and we start getting all deep, and she's like 'you said something was up?' and she tosses her hair so it flicks out and over her back and then she turns to me with

63

her serious face, and I know. It's time. So I prep. I take a deep breath like I'm struggling, and I'm like 'Umm, yesterday I… Um, something happened. Something really bad happened'.

And she's there. None of this breathless, chick bullshit, she's just there. And she takes my hand in her hands, and she says 'tell me.' So I tell her.

*He is still for a moment, then begins.*

It was after we went for gelato. After I waited with you for your bus for like forty-five minutes in the rain. After that I walked home in the rain. But by the time I got home I was in a freaking sick mood, all little tiny rain bits over my jumper and on my arm hairs and shit. Anyway so I walk up the path of my house and suddenly everything shifts. I start getting this really weird feeling, I dunno. I get it a bit, like I'm walking along and I kinda get this sense that a car crash is going to happen on the road next to me or whatever. Do you get that? So anyway I'm walking up my path, and I'm all 'something's wrong' but then logically I'm like 'shut up you mug, nothing's fucken wrong.' So I ring the doorbell. Yeah Mum doesn't let me have keys to the house. So I ring the doorbell, and I'm just kinda standing there with this growing feeling of, like, fuck fuck fuck, like I really need to piss all of a sudden, and shit, and run, and yell, so I yell, I yell out, I'm like 'Hello?!' and there's no response, only I think I can hear Mum moving around in the house, so I figure maybe she has headphones on or some shit, listening to her fucken audio books—anyway so I go around the side of the house. I go around… [*MICHAEL breathes heavily*] the side—sorry—of the house, I go through the gate and say hey to Bluey, only she's not there, and by this stage I'm fucken wired, because Bluey is *always* there when I open the back gate, fucken best dog.

So I close the gate.

And I walk up the side of the house, and I'm all 'Bluey? Bluey, come on girl' and she's not coming, but then I get around to the back of the house and the back door's already open, which is weird, and Bluey's little head is poking out through the door, which is also weird, because she's lying down, and not moving, and her neck is way smaller than it should be, and it's kindof across the doorstep, which is red, and there's dark red leeching into the straw doormat, a lot of it, and I think the red's coming from Bluey, and I think 'hey, red, coming out of Bluey! Red, blue!' and I chuckle, and then I vomit. I don't even really remember recovering from that either, I'm kinda just vomiting, and then I'm stepping over Bluey and running into the house, the kitchen, past the groceries on the counter, and I'm all 'What the fuck Mum, what happened to Bluey?!' but she's not in the back room, not in the kitchen, not in the TV room, not in my room, and there were groceries on the counter.

In the kitchen, there were groceries on the counter.

Something *is* wrong.

And I'm standing in front of mum's door. And the hall is dark. And the door is dark, dark wood. And in all the darkness it takes me a moment to actually find the door-handle, but once I do I just go straight for it, I just go straight in, and... Yeah, and there she is. Mum's home, she's on her bed. Lying on her back, but face down. Twisted, arms twisted, twisted, she's all twisted, twisted, twisted, twisted, all I can see are twists, and all I can hear in my head is the word twist until the word twist becomes completely meaningless, and then still, twist, twist, twisted, twist, twists, twist, twist, twist, the letters, twist, T-W-I-S-T, twist, my mum, twisted, and so still.

> *Big silence. Michael resumes slowly, reveling for a while in the silences.*

And I finish it like that, just silent for ages.

Kayley sitting there, listening to my silence, like she wanted to be completely sure I'd finished.

She bought it, she fully did. And she was all 'I'm glad you called me,' and then she went straight in. Boom. I mean, for a kiss, but I just... man, kiss isn't even the fucken word, it sounds like an insult. She was so soft, I could feel the muscles moving under our lips, together. But then we were apart again, and her eyes. Her eyes! You ever looked into a girl's eyes before? I mean you've looked at them, but looking into them. The colour was completely irrelevant, she was just letting me straight into the black bits, the pupils. And then she just reels off this poem. Whole thing, start to finish, this awesome poem about this dude who sails out to sea in this sweet boat made of bones or some shit, and when she finishes I'm all 'Who wrote that?' and she's like 'I did'.

This is ridiculous, man. I just thought she'd be a great lay—which, by the way, she was—but we were… It was just us. And her hair was all getting in my face and in our mouths, but we didn't care because every little touch reminded us that we were still alive. Our eyes were open even when our mouths were open and we cried the same tears, we held each other like breath, we touched nothing but one another. And after, I don't even know. Like when I get home, I'm gonna have a look in Mum's room to check that she isn't lying dead on the bed, that she's still away on holiday because last night she was dead. I know she wasn't, but she was. And this morning didn't feel any different. And Kayley made the best pancakes! Holy fuck, dude, they're like fucken massive clouds of breakfast heaven! She's everything! She's so… She's— And I can't lose this one, not with mum rocking up and Kayley finding out and everything fucking up, man, you've got to help me kill her.

    *Long pause.*

Mum, not Kayley. Fuck, not Kayley, dickhead. I've got it all sorted, I just don't know if I can move the body on my own.

I think Bluey'll be fine. I don't want to get rid of her. I will if I have to though.

    *Pause.*

You're gonna help me with this, yeah?

# Hunger

## Brooke Robinson

*Sam, 17*
*A restaurant kitchen.*

**SAM:**

Gas flames
dishes stacked
added to
more orders!
In my uniform so bleached I could disappear
I'm still chopping the red stuff
TABLE 5 COMING
concentrate
vertical strokes
(just like you)
my knife slips
shit
splats on the floor
I'LL CLEAN IT UP
I bend down
sop up the red
no room to move
in single file
my shoes touching with those of the next kitchen hand
I level back up to the stove
my head catches a saucepan handle as I rise
oh god
not again

tossed over

the pan soars

liquids slop

the whole kitchen quakes with fear

NEXT ORDER

IT'S COMING

spoon to lips

taste

tongue around

latch onto that layer of

nothing

I... can't

nothing left

keep stirring

IT'S COMING

you grunt

spittle in the air

no time

stir

what

what's that

a red drop crawls along the inside of the saucepan

IT'S COMING I SAID

the red inches down

before I can act

hits the surface of the liquid

and spreads

blood

oh shit!

flip over my hands

burns

Hunger

scabs

thick skin

the usual

eyes off the stove

you hit me across the back of the head

My neck snaps

a cut

there

a hole in my left arm

you grab the saucepan handle

rip it off the heat

dip the spoon in

push it to your ruddy face

no

no

no

what are you doing

you can't

I NEED FIVE MORE MINUTES

you shake your head

please

you're not listening

no

you can't take that out

IT'S NOT READY

I...

you turn to face me

YOU WHAT

I suck in some air

nothing

It's fine

get it out there

shit

food lapped onto two plates

I hold my breath

look up through the skylight in the kitchen ceiling

just for a second

We're not supposed to do this but you're not looking so I stick my head round into the dining room

shoulders hunched my four fingers grip the wall

I'd forgotten how white the room is all walls, clean tablecloths and crockery

the smell of pale roses

I watch the waiter glide over to two women at the corner table

I look down at the cut in my arm and a new droplet of blood pauses between skin and floor

the jaws of the women slacken and slide for what feels like infinity

as a black crust forms over my lungs and I can't keep going on like this

I just need to breathe

and

then

she smiles

the older of the two women smiles

she digs her spoon back in deep

masticates

swallows

and smiles again

my lungs relax

it's fine

you didn't see the blood

they didn't taste the blood

kitchen sounds burrow inside

# Hunger

white noise of

silver on silver

and the slow peel and burn of the lacquer on the bottom of
saucepans

standing next to me

your skin cooled to a rare soft pink

nice

you say

good work

they told the waiter

the women

compliments to the chef

they want more

table 7 and 8 overheard and want to order it too

Three minutes, you bark

Ok

Keep stirring

oh god

that means

it was

the blood

no

TWO MINUTES KID

no

no

I can't

that

I

ONE MINUTE

no

shit

do something

recipe

red stuff

heat

green stuff

spoon in

taste

it's empty

it's nothing

I

can't do this

I

can't

do

it

you're

standing close

you're smiling but your hand is raised and it sweeps through the air,
I flinch instinctively as your hand swoops and stops to a

sudden

pat

on my shoulder

the three layers of fabric between your palm and my shoulder
unravel to thread and I can feel your skin on mine

it's my blood

my insides you want and you don't even know it

I trace my index finger around the cut on my arm

the edges bend

release

one

two

# Hunger

three drops into the saucepan

stir it in clockwise

that's it

no more

that's all I've got to give

IT'S READY

you snatch at the saucepan and the plates disappear

MORE KID MORE

your lips apart

teeth jutting out

but I'm not scared

the others

muted

the kitchen

silent

I grab extra saucepans

fire up all the hot plates

have four going at once

nobody's looking

paw at my arm wound

do ten drops in each saucepan

spoon slashing a figure eight between pans one, two, three, four

I'm losing a lot of blood now

hold on to the side of the bench

my weight skids

away from me

catch sight of my arm

the outline erased

bunch up my uniform and see the arm flesh is… faded

MORE ORDERS KID YOU'RE DOING GREAT

more blood leaks and drips to the floor

a sticky pool underfoot

but my shoes

not in the mess

they're

hovering

slightly

in the air

ankle height

resting on an invisible shelf

COME ON I'M WAITING

air escapes my lungs

Snap!

I'm heavy again

my feet drop to the floor

back to work

Plates lined up

gleaming and perfect

catch your eye thrown back at me in the surface of a pan

the way you're looking

at me

you're happy

you're actually proud

new saucepans

new spoons

even before I start stirring

hang my arm over the pan

a transparent limb now

feather-light

pour in a cup of my secret ingredient

MORE

circling above my head

# Hunger

stirring

all the way up to the skylight in the ceiling

I cover the pots

let them simmer

I want to see their faces!

lean my head out the back door to the outdoor seating area

An elderly couple

eating my dish

deep smiles across both faces

I smile back and wave

but my arm

doesn't actually raise

a shadow moves but the flesh and bone

I can't budge

can't control it

I spy the next table of diners

nodding and chewing

a helium balloon reads: HAPPY BIRTHDAY

it hovers near a gas heater by a little girl

WHERE'S THE FOOD BOY

stirring again, both pans

I dish it out

new batch

simmering

the blood's still dripping from my cut

but the red has gone out of it

DONE!

out of the back window my eye catches the little girl's birthday
balloon

it bobs up and down but always comes to still lower than it began

some helium has leaked out

I feel

taller

myself

lighter and

free

as if the helium has leeched through to me

and YES

I look down

my feet

not touching the ground

I kick my legs

reach up and rise another few centimeters

the balloon drops again

as if a counter weight

instantly I rise another few centimeters

the balloon lowers further towards the ground I rise upward, keeping the balance of things

you leave the kitchen for the outside dining area

I call out, point down with my toes but you can't hear me or see me I'm floating too high up now far beyond your reach

There's a grey smudge in your hand

a fork

you approach the table with the little girl but your knee buckles and you trip

lose your balance for a moment and the fork runs straight into the balloon

POP!

it sinks

dead

I SOAR

alive

I can't stop it now

## Hunger

I'm
higher
under my skin I feel my blood heated to boiling point
but a gentle boil from liquid to vapor and now it's free

# The Circle of Life

## Alice Cooper

*The stage is set with two piles of clothes downstage. One contains a white shirt and trousers, the other the same, but for a four year old. Two boxes of shoes—one large, one small sit adjacent to each pile.*

*Liam 17, dressed in boxers and socks, walks on stage holding a glass of milk. He sits down and places the glass in front of him, as if for someone else.*

**LIAM:**

There you go.

> *He picks up the child's black trousers and pulls out the needle already pinned to the pants.*

Okay. Let's give this a go.

> *He attempts to thread the needle. He misses first, then gets it.*

Yes!

> *He ties a knot in the thread and pushes it through the fabric. He begins hemming the cuffs, figuring out how to sew as he goes.*

> *Calling offstage*

Yeah, down soon!

> *Silence.*

Dad and I really miss hearing you.

You're such a good talker.

You have the best stories.

And so smart, too—

Such a clever brother—

*I* didn't even know the difference between Spiderman and Superman when I was your age, but you, you could have your own TV show!

And when you explained to mum that December was a rainforest—showing her a picture of it on the calendar—that was amazing.

And your singing—

*Calling offstage*

Yes, Dad just give us a min!

*Silence. Still sewing.*

Hey, Bill. You remember we watched the Lion King?

You remember the scene with all the buffalo running together in that huge group? And how there were so many of them and they were going so fast that Simba's dad gets trapped, squished in the middle and then doesn't wake up again? And Simba gets really sad?

Well.

That's kind-of what happened.

To Mum, if mum was a lion.

*Liam laughs.*

I mean—she wasn't trampled! But, after, after the buffalo have been past and Simba walks over to his dad and sees him—she was like that—a bit like Simba's dad in that—she, she, she couldn't get up, anymore.

*Calling offstage.*

Yes Dad!

But she didn't fall. Not like you fall off your bike, or me off my skateboard, but—

*Silence. Picks up the needle again continuing to sew.*

Aunty Jenny and Tom are going to come over tonight—

Said she's going to bring your favourite; lasagna.

*Liam places the trousers down.*

There you go. All done. Not bad eh?

Okay, pop them on. Like me.

*Liam proceeds to get dressed, starting with his trousers.*

C'mon pop your trousers on.

Please.

C' mon Bill, Dad's waiting.

Please Bill. Just copy—

Billy you're gonna have to get dressed.

Billy. Clothes. On. Now.

> *To offstage*

Yes, we're coming Dad!

Billy. Just. Put. On. Your. Clothes.

Look, just stop being such a fucking little brat and put your bloody clothes on so we can get in the car and get this shitty day over with. No one wanted mum to die, but that's what's happened and we all have to deal with it including you. Okay. So just—put your shirt on.

> *Sighs.*

Sorry.

Sorry.

Sorry Bill.

Sorry, Billy, I didn't mean it—I'm just… I'm just a bit… sad. I miss mum too you know.

Look.

No one *really* wants to go today.

*I* don't want to go.

Right now, I'd like to go into the kitchen and eat Mum's roast chicken with gravy and potatoes and have apple crumble for desert.

But that's the thing about being a big boy; you don't always get what you want.

Today, we have to go to the church.

To say goodbye

And Dad and me and aunty Kathy will tell some stories about mummy and after there'll be flowers and cordial and cake and people will say nice things. Some will say prayers. Not everyone will— Uncle Frank won't— he doesn't believe in God— but some people will.

And, we will sing. We will all sing some songs to make us all feel a bit better. And that's why we thought it would be really cool if you sang too. Sang the one you did for her birthday. Cos we all really loved that. We thought it was really nice. And everyone loves hearing you sing. You're the best singer of all of us—

Hey, why don't we rehearse now?

> *Liam picks up a sock and puts it on his hand and speaks as a sock puppet.*

Hey Billy, I'm Socky and I've heard you're a really great singer—

I saw you sing at the concert last year- you looked so cool up there. I bet you're going to sing even better today— make your mum really proud of you— if I weren't a sock, I'd be singing up there with you— but I suppose I have to go back to my drawer sometimes or the underpants will think I ran away with a shoe!

> *To offstage*

Yeah- we're coming!

> *Takes off sock slowly.*

We gotta go now Bill.

Gotta be a big boy today.

Good Lad. C'mon.

> *Beat. Leaning in to listen.*

What was that? What did you say?

Bob the— Yeah, cause you can!

C'mon.

> *Liam picks up the bundle of clothes and carries them offstage.*

… How does it go again?

Ah, that's it—

> *Singing*

Bob the Builder, can he fix it.

Bob the builder, yes he can…

# The Last Post

## Sarah Gaul

*Rose is standing next to a Port-a-Loo (Port a Loo could be physically onstage, it could be imagined, or indicated by a sign etc). Faint party music in the background. Rose and Ed are at the 'funeral after party' or 'wake' of one of their close friends, Kevin, who drowned in an incident 7 days prior. Rose is holding a shattered iPhone. She speaks into the side wall of the Port-a-Loo.*

## ROSE:

… It's in… five pieces… Ed.

It's gone. I'm really sorry.

When you drop them in water you're supposed to… put them in a bucket of rice… and apparently it absorbs all the moisture? But I dunno if putting all five pieces of it in rice will do much. We could try Tarzan's grip, that really good glue?

> [*Pause*]

[*Sudden realisation*]… Oh Ed, It's all your messages from Kev… and all your photos…

> [*She looks closely at the pieces*]

Maybe I can rescue your SIM card.

I think it's been a really good day, Ed, don't you reckon? I mean, I thought it would be one of those things where there is a choir and just those shitty assorted cream biscuits, and I thought everyone would be wearing that kind of black that says 'I can't laugh today.'

But a cover band? Really? And beer? And are there normally… after parties?

Mr. Hamm was saying it's 'what Kevin would have wanted.' But Ed, I reckon what Kevin would have wanted is to not be lying in a box at his own party. But he WOULD encourage the binge drinking. He'd be lining up shots on his own coffin. Because tequila and grief are best friends.

*Speaks into the side wall of the Port-a-Loo*

And it's supposed to be me locking myself in the toilet at these events, Ed. I'm the girl. Don't be such a woman… Ed? [*Knocks on the side of the Port-a-Loo. No response*] Eddie? Ed! Are you… are you alright? Oh have you got your period, Eddie? Ed come on, just open the door.

*Listens a little longer, perhaps shuffling is heard*

Hey… the speech. What you would have said at his 21$^{st}$. It was funny. I liked it. I think I liked the present tense. At such a past tense event it had a ring to it. All the Is's and does's and can's. They were nice. Better than what Father Andrew said. Kev didn't even like Father Andrew.

Does anybody like Father Andrew?

He hobbled after Kev for like four blocks and phoned the cops the other weekend coz he thought Kev was pissing on a gravestone… Which he was. But now this weekend the asshole is up there talking about how 'noble' and 'loyal' Kev is. As if he's NOT going to piss on KEV'S gravestone the first chance he's got.

*Pauses and listens*

Hey Ed, you know his Facebook page is still running? All these people have posted Simpsons quotes and 'you would've's' and 'if you were here nows.' All in hypotheticals. All stuff that no one would ever say to Kev's face because he'd think it was heaps gay, wouldn't he?… But I think those messages might be for us all. It's how we say, 'Look, hey look… I'm grieving too.'

I scrolled down to his last status update. 8 days ago. His final recorded words: 'LOL HIDE YOUR WEED. Mama ALWAYS knows… OH SHIIIIIIITTTTT exclamationmarkexclamationmarkexclamationmark.' His last words. The unholy last post. And his last picture is him dressed as a stripper at the footy dinner, did you see it? Rest in peace, you weed-smoking trannie. Only Kevin, Ed. Only Kev could do that… and still not look gay. [*She takes tissues from her bag and dabs her eye. She then looks across the lawn*]

Hey Ed, um, it looks like Mrs. Hamm needs a hand with the sausage rolls and party pies… do you reckon we could go over and help?

*No response*

Hey Ed, it… really looks like she needs our help. [*Knocks on the side again*] Eddie?

… Did you see Alex earlier? In a… suit. I dunno, three days after it happened, Alex turns to me in the canteen line at lunch, after three days of not really talking to anyone, and says [*urgently*] 'Kev always ate their barbecue chips—he always ate them, so lets buy all their barbecue chips today.' [*Beat*] And turns back around and doesn't say anything to me until we've eaten nineteen packets of barbecue chips each. I feel sick, like a potatoey kind of too-much-salt sick, I feel sick, and the whole time we are thinking about that word 'ate' that isn't 'eat' but it couldn't be 'eat' because Kev can't eat anymore.

And have you talked to Ryan since it happened? I walked past the park on the way home last night. Ryan was there in the middle of the field, with a whole bunch of footballs sitting on the ground. He was kicking them into the trees one by one. And then just standing.

And staring.

And waiting. For a really long time.

And then, without taking his eyes off the trees, he'd reach down and get another footy and kick it.

We've all been doing it. The waiting.

Maybe Ryan ignores the past tense. The 'not' of it. The Not-being. That absence that we'll all fill with COULD. That maybe if you kick the footy far enough into the trees, it could come arcing back out. The 'maybe' and most of all the WOULD. That strange kind of joy and… self-loathing… when you wonder what he would have said if he was just looking over your shoulder or on the other end of the phone.

Did you… write on his page Ed? I didn't. What if one day I open Facebook over breakfast and he's online? What if I talk to him and he… talks back?

Maybe it's not heaven, maybe it's cyberspace.

Because it doesn't exist in this world. You just have blind faith that it exists somewhere because you can see it lit up on your screen. But it doesn't physically exist. And now Kevin doesn't either... what if they all DON'T exist in the SAME PLACE?

[*Excited*] Like when you post something to Facebook and it just never, it just never shows up on their wall. Or... or you send a text that just never arrives. And you send a funny picture email but the picture, the picture never gets there... Ed...

...What if the dead just reach out and... catch them because they think it's funny. Or they are bored, or lonely.

[*Cautiously, tearfully*] Hey Ed... what would Kevin say if he saw you holed up...in a ladies' Port-a-Loo... at FATHER ANDREW'S church... on a Saturday?

He'd call you a homo, Ed.

He'd think you were a real dickhead for leaving all your friends outside in the cold. He'd get his Leatherman and cut a Kev-sized hole in the door and come in there with you. [*Her frustration and upset builds, bashes on the door, throws her weight against it*] Ed. Eddie. EDDIE! You've GOTTA COME OUT ED!! LISTEN TO ME ED LISTEN TO ME COME OUT OF THERE or at LEAST just... let me in ... [*fumbles frantically with the iPhone*] We'll fix it, Ed, we'll... glue it back together, we'll fix it, we'll fix him. [*Puts the iPhone pieces on the ground, pulls an earring out of her ear and uses it to remove the tiny, fiddly little SIM card. She sits, relieved. Pause*]

... I've got him. I've got it. Your... SIM card. Its ok, Ed. Your SIM card's fine. I'm holding it my fingers... right here. We'll find him another phone.

[*She puts her earring back in, tucks the pieces of the phone away in her bag. Pauses. Deep sadness as she watches something in front of her*] Alex and Ryan are wandering around like they've walked into the wrong church. I dunno, Ed. It's 'another death in another town' and everyone points their finger to boredom and alcohol and breakdown of law and order. But it's an old story. I think people would just sip their coffee and glance over the headline and scroll past. Because it's been done before. The drinking and the drowning. But in a month, three months, five months, what happens?

How do we look at each other over the top of our computer screens and say 'this... thing... that happened to us all... is still happening.'

Because people forget and the newspaper forgets.

But Facebook never forgets.

Ed… in a year or six months Facebook will remind me to 'Reconnect with Kevin. Say Hello!'

> *Pause*

I don't know what I'd do, Ed.

> *Slow fade to black.*

# La Conversación

## Alexandra Macalister-Bills

*Hostel dorm room full of bunk beds. It's messy, beds unmade, backpacks propped about. In the centre a girl of nineteen searches haphazardly through her bag. She is on the phone but using a hands free headset.*

Yeah I got your messages, yes all of them.

Yesterday

I haven't had time. I don't have time.

I'm on my way to a gig. It's called La Bamba. La Bamba!

Let me

Let me finish what I was saying. It's this 12 Piece African Drumming Improvisation Group. It's in an abandoned warehouse,

No of course I'm not avoiding you.

Quick. Say 'G'day' for my friend from Portugal. I told him you'd be more ocka than me cause I spent those two weeks in the city and you've never lived away from home. I'll put you on—

Come on sis, please?

> *To the room*

Sorry chica

She doesn't want to

I know right total party pooper!

Belle?

No seriously I haven't—

Oh My Gosh! Give me a chance to explain. It's just been so intense here. I spent all day yesterday at a massive hippy market outside this cemetery. It's in this posh barreto, that's suburb in Spanish. I'm learning real quick. Oh yeah and the cemetery is all crypts, mausoleums or whatever the word is. They're all lined up in rows like streets.

It reminds me of when we were little and Mum would make villages out of boxes for us before—

Hold on, hold on

*She puts the phone down and changes her top quickly*

I'm back

Yeah and there's some really old coffins in the crypts, so old they're splitting and the dust is starting to leak out between the boards. I keep wondering if the cats—

*To the room*

Yo chicos what's cat in Spanish?

Gato?

Gato. Sweet.

*Returns to phone*

Stray gatos, they're everywhere. I keep wondering if they sneak through the gaps for a quick snack on whatever grisly meat's left. Though I suppose there'd only be bones left.

What

No

How is that insensitive?

She's getting cremated.

Fine

Fine.

Sorry.

Well this market is full of wooden gourds for maté, herbal tea stuff they drink here. It looks pretty suss the way they drink it, like a cup full of weed but it's only caffeine.

No

No

I told you I wouldn't touch anything here.

*Covers the phone, to the room*

Can you tell the others not to tag me in those photos from La Paz?

Are you there sis?

Yeah so I'm walking around and I can hear this music. I realise I'm humming along and I'm like what is that? It turns out there's this festival soon and that band you kept playing over and over at Easter, umm hang on… Vampire Weekend! That's it, Vampire Weekend, doing a sound check!

Isn't that awesome!

But you love Vampire Weekend.

Yeah

Yeah

I'll email back soon.

Did you even listen? Vampire Weekend!

I know, I know.

Isn't this costing you a fortune?

Well, if Dad's paying.

Wait. Did you see the photo's I put on Facebook? I've taken like 4000 already and I've only been here two weeks! I've already added 30 new friends too. Stalk them.

What was that?

I can't hear. The traffic's epic.

Wait still can't hear you

No. I can't shut the window cause it's sweltering, I'm sweating like that old nurse, that one Mum kept thinking was her sister with caterpillar eyebrows?

That one!

How is that not funny?

Look I told you I can't talk right now

I'm busy

I—

My friends are waiting for me

Of course I know it's Monday. I'm not lying. Just things are different here. Everything happens at night. It's their culture here-

You don't understand what it's like. It's not like there's one poxy pub like at home. There's so much to do. So much I want to do. I've kept souvenirs from everything, tickets, receipts, wrappers—

No

Stop.

I told you I have to go. They'll leave without me.

Hang on.

> *To the room*

Sweet tune! But can you pretty please turn it down?

Cheers.

> *Returns to phone*

I don't care

You decide

It's not like it matters

Don't kid yourself. She's gone

I know what you're doing. I can't. I literally just got here.

Yes yes I'm here but

I don't have time to discuss this.

I

told

you

why

I

> don't

>> know

>>> when

>>>> not

>>>>> now

Wha—

Belle, are you there? Hello?

Hello?

I'll take photos for you

Of course you'll want to see

# La Conversación

*To the door*

Has anyone seen my camera?

I swear I left it—

No, no, it's just my sister babbling away

I'll be super duper quick

It's going to be awesome. Fiesta!

*Returns to phone*

No I was talking to all my friends.

This trip is already so much better than I thought

Oh gross!

Yuck

I think I stepped in someone's toenail clippings. They're all yellow, thick, twisted

Who does that?

Seriously.

I'm not ignoring you. How's Tim. Tell him—

You're making a big deal out of noth—

This isn't a funeral. It's body disposal. We said our goodbyes years ago.

I told you I have to go. Mis amigos are waiting.

*To the door*

Si, si, un momento, por favor!
Belle, I can't. It's too expensive.

It's too far

It's too soon

We talked about this before I left. I know we didn't think it would happ—

but it did.

You can't pay

I wouldn't make it in time.

What would I do after, back home again? Pack peaches at SPC?

I don't even need to be there. Neither do you. Come join me. You need a holiday. Leave Tim behind. Or bring him. Whatever. I told you about all the cute boys? So cute. Except, what's with all the Argentinians having rat's tails? They have sooo much potential You need to see all this. You need to—

Don't guilt trip me! You know how much I did for her.

*Over her shoulder*

Yeah I'm okay chica. I'm
I'm fine. Totally fine.

*She moves to a corner.*

Even if I could leave I have other obligations now.

Yes

Yes I do

I have that volunteering.

At the yoga farm.

Don't get all narky.

At least they'll actually notice if I don't show up

She never knew.

It's been years since she recognised us.

She was a vegetable.

Remember?

> A carrot in a coma
>
> A baked broccoli
>
> A zombie zucchini

I'm not heartless. I'm realistic.

Don't cry, sis,                           deep      breaths

Please?

I'm sorry I didn't call back. I'm sorry I haven't helped organise anything. I'm sorry I'm not there. I know I should be, but—

I can't

I can't

Don't you understand?

La Conversación

I'm not as strong as you
I won't
I won't be able to watch
                    watch them put her in a box.
It's too much                it's too hard            it's too—
Hello? Hello?
Fuck
Fucketty fuck. What's Spanish for fuck?
This phone's speaking to me in Spanish.
Does anyone speak Spanish?

                                        Hablo, Hablas ingles?

What the hell does that mean?
Oh shit I hate languages
Speak slower!

                                            Un poco!
                                        No entiendo!

I don't understand what you're saying!

                                        Por favor!

Sis can you hear me?
Someone tell me what's happening!
Yes it's roaming
Greedy Fuckwits!
Hang on
You're there? Shit sorry, did you hear all that? My phone is eating
credit, precious pesos!
Thanks for looking after everythi—
What
What did
Don't
Don't say that
That's

That's not fair

I        have    to      go.

Wait. Wait. What did she say?

She didn't

She did not!

I don't believe you. That's impossible. I spoke to her before I left. She couldn't tell. She could never tell.

Don't say that! I'm going to come back and—


It can't be that bad. You were ready. You said you were ready. You told me you were ready. You told me you could handle it. You swore—

Don't push me, stop asking me, I can't

I can't

I can't

no

NO

No

Don't make this about us

It's about her

                  her

                        her

Go on.

Say it.

I will.

It's about her

                                                    Mum

                        MumMumMumMumMum

But she isn't, is she?

She wasn't, was she?

You can't say good-bye to someone who's been gone for years

## La Conversación

I can't do this now
I have to go
No
Now
            Tomorrow
maybe                    tomorrow
I'll take photos of the gig for you.

# STICK

## Carolyn Burns

*A typical local community hall. Louise, dressed in her school uniform, sits in a chronic disease support group. She is holding a short wooden rod and a glass of water, from which she periodically sips.*

## LOUISE:

So I've got five minutes? Okay.

I've got the talking stick.

What am I supposed to talk about?

> *Pause.*

What about this weather we've been having?

> *Pause.*

Do I have to talk for the whole five minutes?

> *Pause.*

Mum's annoying.

There's that.

She keeps reminding me to take my pills, like, in the middle of the day, when I don't need reminding, because I take them before breakfast and with breakfast and before bed.

It's fine, she's just worried. She's been shvitzing since I was diagnosed. But it's her own fault, she got onto Wikipedia the other day, and there are all sorts of graphic photos of medical shit on there.

She told me she was just going to look up my prescriptions, but then she started clicking on all these other conditions and diseases, you know where they have that list of side effects? And then they have all these horrible pictures of like gangrene and, I don't know, eczema, and by the time I got back from school she was, like, reading about compound fractures and she knew all of this statistical information on the relationship between credit swaps in Iceland and

96

the financial crisis, and when she told me what she'd done I was like 'You nerp! Wikipedia owns!'

Then she started crying.

I told her not to cry because it's not like it's fatal, and there's really effective medicine now, and I might not need a colostomy bag for ten years anyway, but then she started crying even more. I don't know why she was crying; I'm the one who's going to end up shitting in a bag.

Like I said, she's a total nerp.

*Pause.*

On Saturday last week I couldn't get to sleep because the pain was pretty bad and I couldn't keep my codeine down, so Dad just sat next to me on the couch and recited all the American Presidents in order, from memory.

That was random.

He knows the numbers, too. Grover Cleveland's both twenty-two and number twenty-four because he served non-consecutive terms. I think Dad just wanted to talk about stuff, but he didn't know what to say, so he just talked. When he went up to bed he patted me on the shoulder and said, 'Franklin Roosevelt was elected president three times, and he was a proper cripple.'

Franklin Roosevelt was number thirty-two.

*Pause.*

Am I supposed to talk about my feelings? I don't know, I'm good. I feel good.

*Pause.*

My feelings about being sick?

I don't really have any feelings about being sick, but I have thought of a slogan for you guys, if you'd like to hear it?

Crohn's and Colitis Australia: life's shit and then you die.

Not cool?

I've got one about schizophrenia, too: 'All my friends keep telling me I'm crazy.'

*Pause.*

That's not funny.

*Pause.*

Maybe it should be 'All our friends keep telling *us* we're crazy.'

*Pause.*

People with epilepsy are pretty funny.

*Pause.*

Maybe next time we could mix this whole thing up a bit. We could invite people who've got other things stuffed up with them and then we could all have a chat and maybe then we'd all feel better about ourselves, because, you know, I mean, yesterday I was a bit sad because I really want to go to Cambodia and now I can't get travel insurance, but, if we had epileptic people here, I might feel better because at least I can go to a rave, you know, if I ever start liking techno music.

And they'd feel better too, because, let's face it, we're revolting.

Maybe I could swap diseases with an epileptic who likes dancing and toilets.

*Pause.*

You said before that there isn't anything that's too stupid to share with the group, so I'll just say it. You'll think I'm nuts, but I've got the talking stick, so you can all just go get stuffed.

It was like eight weeks ago, just after I found out, the day after my endoscopy it was, which, *by the way*, when I woke up, hurt like I'd been deep-throating a screwdriver… What was I saying?

Oh, yeah, it was just after I found out about, yeah, and I'm walking back from the bus stop, slowly, 'cause I was tired, and I started to get this weird sensation in my foot, like there was something *in there*.

So I sit down on a wall, and take my right shoe off and I shake it, but nothing comes out. And it was weird, because there was nothing in my *shoe*, but there was a rock in my *foot*—inside, right under the skin, like, under the sole of my right foot.

What was strange about this rock, if it makes sense for there to be just one strange thing about a rock just hanging out inside your foot, was that it was perfectly round. Like a small marble, trapped just beneath the surface of the skin.

It was small that day, it started out small. It's bigger now. The size of a golf ball in my heel, but smooth, not dimpled. I can show you. You can touch it if you like.

*She puts the rod and the glass of water on the floor and takes off her right shoe, then, distracted:*

You'd think I'd worry about it—but I'm not worried. I like it. Every time my right foot hits the ground I feel it roll slightly under the skin—against the bone, like a hinge, or a wheel.

I take a step and it slips. I take another step and it slips again.

The little stone speaks to me as it rolls. 'Keep going,' it tells me.

I step and it slips.

'Keep going!'

And I keep going.

Is that weird? I don't really care if it's weird, stuff weird.

They told me that I'd be getting sick, but actually I'm just getting awesome.

*Pause.*

Sure, I'm anemic. I'm tired. I can't get much sleep because when I lie down, I throw up. I've got a bucket beside my bed and I don't even bother getting up to brush my teeth after anymore, 'cause it'll just happen again. The other night I threw up so much that the bile I was spewing was bright yellow, like a highlighter, and then it turned pink, with the blood. But Dad says that, from a distance, it sounds a bit like I'm laughing when I vomit.

I know, my immune system is too strong and it's making my body try to eat itself, sure. But what if it isn't?

What if I'm actually changing? I think I might be. My elbows are feeling strange. My shins are itchy. The back of my skull feels a bit smoother than usual, actually, and when I press it, my scalp just slides over the surface.

So I have this idea: I think I might be turning into glass.

*Pause.*

I think that all my bones and all my muscles and skin might be turning into glass—really hard and smooth and clear. Fragile, yeah, but heaps strong.

*Pause. She picks up the rod.*

Who wants the talking stick?

# Senseless

## Alex Cullen

*A messy teenage bedroom. Warm light floods in. Anna, 18 locks the door. She goes to her school bag, pulls out a tattered book with loose sheets. She spreads them before her, holds her iPod to her mouth. Hits record.*

## ANNA:

Mum, you're in the kitchen, chopping, grating. The house alive with noise.

When you lose sound do you lose the memory of it?

Do songs get stuck in your memory, mozzie net droning, loops of verse cycling your brain like hum-sickness?

Finger ballet. Sam signs with me. My fingers are a messy tango, all twisted up. What kind of music plays in Sam's head that makes her hands dance like that?

You test me on what I can hear. You mutter, 'Rhubarb, rhubarb, hum, murmur, murmur.' Dad plays jazz and I can tell it's jazz even when it's down low because of your face.

Little sis practises dance in her room. She plays the music too loud. I hear it as I drift off to sleep, poking at my ear, gaining entrance to my brain.

Sam says she still hears music, but distorted. She thought the car starting was a dog's bark. She thought the photocopier was her mum yelling from downstairs.

Will I lose your voice?

When you move your lips will I 'hear' your lisp through sight?

Is it synaesthesia, do you hear with sight? Can you taste sound? And then when you lose sound is that taste as light and fragrant as rose water, is it sweet and diluted like cordial, or is it a mouldy biscuit, stale and growing fur under the collapse of memory?

*She shifts her notes.*

Aloneness, sleep—I drift to consciousness, a bite in my stomach that travels to my brain and eyes. The lurch of dread lifts me off my bed, makes my heart race with chunder and sick streaming through me like a half crushed cocktail, rocks of ice slamming around in my gut.

Snap my fingers by my ear.

*Snap.*

My feet return to Earth.

The day comes with a stale smear of relief. Day, which nobody tells you about, when you ask yourself how much of the world might have gone? What has stolen away in the darkness? You attempt, in your head, to detail that scope, readjusting loose thoughts to measurements and scales.

Scrape, shuffle, scuff.

And where does this voice go now? Does it live in my iPod, curled up, waiting for someone else's ears to slide into? Your ears, years from now, when my diction's gone soft and my voice is too loud—will you play this and hear me? This very me, right now.

Will you hear me changing?

Take the bus. Every day. I'll sit next to the window, lay my forehead on the glass and feel reverberations through my skull, my nose and chin and cheeks vibrating until my face is tingly.

But then the brush of hairs against arm and the smell—the salty, dampened rush of sweat as a guy presses against me, dressed in some kind of poly-nylon nightmare, purples and reds and blacks, and his hair is thick and wet with slick. Cigarettes, blunt fingernails.

Bashing his knee into mine,

his legs so far apart,

like a gymnast doing the splits,

baggy parachute pants sagging—expensive leg tarp.

On my side. My side of the seat.

His knee banging into mine. Pot hole, bang. Red light, bang.

Fucking wanker, fucking move.

I bash my knee right into his.

Bang.

His mouth explodes with rushed angry words that float like bubbles and pop. The sound of the bus, the engine swallowing me, my mind mechanics, gears, stalling. Bump.

He's looking at me, waiting. Plastic chain and Lynx, he looks at me like he knows that something's not there...

It's not my stop, but I stand. His mouth still moving—the words I catch 'You... nothing wrong... spaz.'

I climb over him—a mountain of knees, fist on red button punch, he doesn't move his legs, but spreads them further. One leg over. His knee jabs the back of mine. I want to howl.

But it's OK, Mum. I'm fine. I get out and walk and I make it in time for the train.

But playing in my mind is the rough lick of his voice. 'Spaz' brands itself into me, absorbing into brain tissue and diluting the stream of my mind. It's his voice that stays in my head. Not mine. Not the sound of the house, not the chopping or jazz, not the door sliding, not you calling out my name.

One day I'll speak and not hear myself. I'll never be able to listen to this again.

Sam and Francis sign on the way to school. The second carriage on the platform is ours, further away from the press of green and navy—colours I swear I'll never wear once I'm in uni. No collars or pleats or ties or itchy jumpers. Sam and Francis converse in rapid pace, I follow their faces and not their hands and I piece fragments together. Kids mimic them, giggling.

When the interpreter stands at the front of the class there is no interest from the others as they stare slack jawed at the teacher, fumbling to jab her USB in a grandmother computer plastered with fading school stickers. The interpreter looks like a teacher, knitted baubles hanging off her cardigan, threads sticking out and floating above the knit, glasses askew from the exuberance of her finger speech.

Our teacher talks rapidly as I try and follow. If I turn my eyes towards paper I miss things—some things, not many yet. I lose the teacher, because she can't get the screen saver to stop, and watch the interpreter, her animated face guiding Sam and Francis, their frowns of concentration evidence of engagement. They do not sit next to me. Nobody sits next to me. The panic in their eyes when I say, 'Hi' reminding me of conversations I've missed. Voices punctuated with pauses made from silence where there should be none. Words that drop from sentences as if the line gave way.

I sit alone.

At home you and Dad exaggerate your words, though I can hear all sound over the serenity of dinner. Little sis slops soup over herself and cries at the scalding. I keep these cries and words locked inside for when the ghost of sound plucks at my memory.

When you go to the kitchen, and Dad to the lounge, and sister to dancing—this is my time. I speak words from books and feel them roll in my mouth, listening to the way they burst, hearing the voice I was born with, that I was given—by you. And I'll always have those words inside me, undiluted, pristine, my own to speak with.

*She lowers the iPod. Turns it off.*

# Ben Thomas, I Love You

## Alysha Herrmann

*Alison, 17. Holds a notebook stuffed with other handwritten letters and cards.*

**ALISON:**

I can't. Can't think.

I want to rip your fucking eyeballs out.

No.

I want to sweep your hair away from your eyes and kiss your cheek like when you were a baby. You. My baby brother. My brother Ben.

I can't find you here. You're not here. This isn't you. Wasn't you.

It wasn't you. It was someone else. This doesn't happen. People with mothers and fathers and brothers and sisters and happy homes.

This doesn't happen.

Did you know I'd seen it? Your book. You said nothing. I said nothing. Now. Now I have to. Say.

But Can't. I can't. Say anything. Something.

I'm burning with it. It's piercing me. You are. You are piercing me. Like him. Like you pierced him. Like then.

Your cheek is so smooth. You're mine. Mine.

> *Softer*

I caught you that time. That time at the beach. You were small. You slipped and I caught you. Now here somehow smaller than I thought. Tiny in this box.

Laughing at me. Leaving me this. Do what with this?

I caught Dad trying to throw everything away. Our moments. Our lives. He had no right. It's mine.

He grabbed me. Yelled in my face and spit was flying everywhere and I slapped him.

I felt relieved. To hit him like that. That satisfying skin on skin sting. It felt good.

He had no right. It's mine. All of it. These things. Even this. Even this is mine. And I won't let anyone throw it away. Have it.

I want to slap you. Rattle you. Shake you. I want to shake you until all your bones clank together like a great giant wind chime of bones. I want to shake you until all your blood is a frothy red milkshake. I want to shake you until my arms fall off. I want to shake you…

awake. Awake. I want to shake you awake.

I want to. Talk. Let's talk. I found it. Words you wrote. Pictures you drew. Sick. Sick and twisted and you. You. Another You. This you. Stick figures and words. Words you. Carve, carve into cheeks. Like your cheek here and it's soft and you're not here. You're not. And now I have it and someone should know. Someone should. I should give it to them. Those people. The ones. Who. Who.

Only minutes to contain you.

Minutes.

Contain you.

You, my brother Ben.

To shoot you down. They said you wouldn't stop. They said they had no choice. I believe them. I saw the pictures and read the words you wrote there.

Different words.

You are the bestest big sister in the whole world. Luvv fromme Ben.

You. At kindy. On Cardboard. Gave those words to me. Made them mine. Like this. You let me find it and that makes it mine.

So now. I can't throw it away like car magazines and porn under your bed. I could throw that away. This though. This is your words. Your written words.

I keep them. Did you know? All of them. All the ones Dad tried to throw away. Our moments. Every letter. Every card. Every scrap of paper with your words scrawled to me. Something treasured. Something mine. You.

This is sick and wrong. Stick figures and cheeks and words dancing under my eyelids. Knowing. Knowing I should let them have it. Should tell them. Should have told them. Might help. Them. Still. Someone. Help that boy even. The one. With legs burnt. Words carved in a pimply cheek. Tiny holes in one shoulder. I see him. Shredded by stick figure pictures and half scrawled notes.

Your smiling face with your scruffy hair on TV and everyone wants to know.

Why.

Haven't told them. I haven't shown them what you wrote or what you drew.

I went in to your room. I was looking for you. Knowing I'd open the door and you'd be laying upside down on your bed dangling a joint from the corner of your mouth and I'd tell you to put the damn thing out before Dad saw it and you'd laugh in that cocky way you had and

None. Of. It. Would. Be. Real.

Now, every word.

Sick and deep and my own agony spilling out of me and trying to catch it and find someplace to keep it.

Something.

Something next.

Keep it.

Have to.

Want to.

Can't.

Shouldn't.

You're sick.

You're fucking sick.

I.

Am.

Sick.

I stopped.

Waited.

Read it.

Waited.

Thought.

Caught the agony.

Quiet.

Quietly.

Everything you ever wrote.

It's mine. I have to keep this.

Because.

Because.

*Beat.*

You're my brother.

# PRINCE WILLY

## Laura Hopkinson

*Lights.*
*Elsa on stage. Party dress? Dressed to kill. For her age. Pink is a big feature. Body glitter beside either eye, and possibly on each shoulder. A motherload of hair clips. She wriggles, impatiently.*

The hot chips are definitely soggy by now.

Disastrous.

Any minute they should be here.
In my actual house.

I stare at the door. My body glitter itches, but beauty is pain.

The doorbell goes.

[*To o/s*] I'VE GOT IT!!!!
I sprint down the hall to the door. My hand hovers over the handle— no one likes a keeno, wait a second, catch my breath.
First impressions are everything.

> *One hand hovers above the invisible door handle, the other smoothes her hair back. The door opens.*

I look up and there she is. She even *smells* like she's famous.
Her nails are really square and hard and shiny.
Her hair is floppy and straight.
She smiles at me with big American movie star teeth.
The teeth from her actual movies.
Her shoes are like hoofs, and she steps aside to reveal: Her Son.

The one who all the body glitter is for.

The one who will be my new best friend.

The One.


And there. He. Is.

He's not quite like I imagined.

My big hurdle here is that he's six. And well, look, the world's just a whole different can of beans when you're eight. You really understand everything on a *deeper* level. I mean I didn't even know I was destined to be an actress until I was seven. Plus I have a pen license now so...

I smile at him for the very first time and he—

Sniffles.

His hair is just as shiny and floppy as hers which is weird because he's a *boy*. It goes around his head like a lampshade.

He looks like a lampshade.

Plus also he reminds me of a suitcase, because of the way his mum has to drag him inside, This way Willy, and heavily he follows her to the kitchen.

I guide them inside, and smell more of her famous-smell. My mum could never smell like this, my mum just smells like detergent. But that won't matter soon. It's time to get to work.

I turn to greet Willy.

> *She smoothes her hair back.*

Hi I'm Elsa.

You must be Willy.

So do you like my body glitter?

It's from the Easter show.

[*Aside*] HE'S A TOUGH ONE!

We're having hot chips tonight. Do you like them? I like them. It's like a feast. Just for us. They got soggy because you were late but I made my dad microwave them.

So he's like a servant.

# Prince Willy

Do you have servants?
He blinks at me twice.
Then once at the ceiling.
Then once at the olives the grown ups are eating.
Then sniffles again.
He says nothing.

It's a wobbly start but the night is young, and so are we.


Dinnertime.

I kindly point at all the crispiest chips in the bowl for him to take and
he does. I'm so thoughtful like that.
I straighten our plastic mats, his has the alphabet on it and animals
for each letter, mine is just a boring one covered in numbers.
I've arranged it this way.

So do you like animals…


I like DINOSAURS.

I love dinosaurs! Maybe when we grow up we can get one for a pet.
Like we could share it, when we're old friends.

They're extincted.

You're so smart. Did you know that I heard that most people who
get homeschooled are actually geniuses. And they can get really rich.
But I guess you already are. Cool.


Again I get nothing.
I watch as each chip turns into a sloppy white mash in his mouth.
He's really showing his age.
It's kind of disgusting.

But I know he'll grow on me over the years.

So at home school, are your teachers all famous people? and instead of maths do you just learn how to be in movies and be famous like your mum?

Do you. you. you have barbeque sauce?

[*Sighs*] This is much trickier than I planned—This is the problem with going after a younger boy.

While I work hard on the conversation, I watch *her* out of the corner of my eye. I watch her tell stories with her hands about the olden days at big school with mum, I watch how she laughs with her lips when she remembers something, I see her feet slip out of her hoof heels under the table and about three times I pretend to go to the toilet so I can spy on the grown ups table on the way.
She takes some of the fish, most of the peas but none of the rice. none of the rice.
From now on, I'm allergic to rice.

When I get back to the kids table for the third time Willy is making finger paintings on his plate with tomato sauce.
My man is getting restless, it's time to assert myself as a woman.

We're going to the TV room.

I close the door behind us and he's found the couch. His Velcro sandled feet dangle off the edge.

Willy there's something I wanna talk about…

He casually wriggles into a starfish. His feet now dangle over the back of the couch and his head hangs upside down over the seat. He stares at a curly piece of chipped paint on the wall.

The kid has no focus, I don't think he'll ever work in film like his mum or I.

Typical man. He's wants me to think he's ignoring me, but I know he feels what I feel.

So Willy. William. I feel like tonight has gone really well, and what I wanted to ask you is, well I

Can we watch Telly?

*She sucks in breath. Then—*

William I WANNA GET MARRIED.

I feel like when you meet the one person you were destined for you need to tell them. You need to tell them in the face.

And see Willy from the moment I first saw you. tonight. I thought, yep. That's my man. What a guy.

So now we just have to make it official. So we can be together forever. And your Mum, she can be with us too.

Because naturally I'd have to move in with you. My friends at school would miss me but they'd understand my career has a much better chance in LA. With you guys.

I was thinking we invite some of your famous friends to our honeymoon—I was thinking Italy—and that way I could set up some good contacts.

Plus also—we can all go swimming and stay up really late and get your servants to bring us ice cream. And we could all just, talk about fashions, or make up dances together, or whatever…

I think your mum would go for it. Plus she can be a bridesmaid so… it's a sweet deal all round.

All we have to do is go into the kitchen and tell the parents. Of our love.

Ready?
William?
Darling?

I'm bored. Can I have more chips?

We finished them
Why can't you make more?
Say you'll marry me.
You're scary
Say.
I'm telling on you
No!
He goes for the door and I see it all of it. My whole career. All
the roles, all the acceptance speeches, my Hollywood mansion in
Disneyland trying to run away. I must stop him. I must stop him. and
I do. The only way I can,

I whack him I hit him I SMACK HIM ON HIS FACE.

His face scrunches up like tin foil because it turns shiny as is gets
wet and I don't think I'll be able to uncrinkle it.
The wet lines from his eyes run into the dribble from him mouth and
the lines run and run into each other and run down and run and run


and I want to run away because all I can see is red cheek skin and wet
eyelashes and all can hear is

*She makes a drawn out croaking sound.*

and I know what's coming—
Big boys don't cry Willy!
—but it's too late, like a wave that's about to hit your boogie board.
Here it comes and—

# Prince Willy

He wails.

Boom the door opens

Mum asks what's happened

Dad looks embarrassed already, asks who's hurt

and worst of all, her

Willy baby what is it?

no nononononono turn off the sound mute him! I look at the telly remote, if only it worked on people, why science why are you so slow!

She hit me

I feel my parents looking at me and it's hurting.

No I didn't

yes, *gasp* you, *gasp* did

Mum's face is next to mine. She says she's very cross, that I have to say sorry. As if I would.

Willy is wrapped in her, *her*, her nails catch the light like sequins as she wipes her thumbs across his cheeks and holds his lampshade head in her hands.

He breathes in to say something else, and he breathes in to say something else and he breathes in to say something else and he. I don't think he's trying to say anything else.

She says she needs her bag

Dad gets it from the kitchen.

She searches with her nails in the bag for—The Puffer.

I feel like helping—look I didn't hit that hard I'm a girl—I step forward to put my hand in and look too but I feel Dad's hand push me back

On my chest and I feel my chest and I see Willy's chest

it's slow now.

Mum says our address to the telephone. I think she's called the police on me. I'm too little for jail. My career is over. My ears they are so hot like my dad has microwave them up.

I stand with my back and hands to the wall. And my knees feel like bendy straws

I feel the one bit of chipped paint on the wall behind me and I really want to rip it off and give it to Willy.

The man and the lady come in and put Willy onto the bed with the wheels and strap him on so they can drive fast. Then they roll him out onto the street into the ambulance car with the lights on top.

She doesn't go back to get her shoes from under the table, she gets into the back barefoot with Dad and the two of them go to hospital. But I'm not allowed.

I don't know what they put on his mouth. Mum what's that for? What's that called?

Why was he like this?

*She weases. She weases.*

I'm stopping. I stopped. I didn't mean to mum.

Mum what happens if.

Will Willy stop too?

Mum.

What is it?

What does that mean?

What does that mean?

What is it?

# AUTHOR BIOGRAPHIES

LACHLAN PHILPOTT

Lachlan Philpott is a Sydney-based writer, dramaturg, teacher and director. His first play *Bison* has had sell-out seasons in Adelaide, Belfast, London, Melbourne and Sydney. His other plays include *Bustown*, *Catapult*, *Colder* (Winner R.E Ross Trust Award 2007), *Due Monday*, *Silent Disco* (Winner Griffin Award for Outstanding New Australian play 2009, Winning Finalist Gap Project Aurora Theatre Co. USA, 2010, short listed Best New Australian Work, The Helpmann Awards, 2011), *Truck Stop* and *The Trouble with Harry*. Lachlan has worked extensively as a writer with Amnesty International. He was also writer in Residence at Red Stitch Theatre, Melbourne in 2006 and Griffin Theatre Company, Sydney in 2010. Lachlan is currently developing the screenplay of *Silent Disco* funded by Screen Australia. He is on the writing team of Starchild Productions new television series *Dungoona*. Lachlan has directed theatre at Australian Theatre for Young People (atyp) and was Artistic Director of Tantrum Theatre, Newcastle between 2003 and 2006. Lachlan co-founded wreckedAllprods with collaborator Alyson Campbell in 2000 and they have regularly produced work in Australia and the UK. Lachlan has taught extensively. Highlights include initiating an Indigenous writing course for Aboriginal students in inner-city Sydney, teaching script writing in Kenya, the UK and The Netherlands. He was the Literary Associate at atyp between 2007 and 2010 where he directed the FRESH INK emerging writers' program.

JASPER MARLOW (*ACL*)

Jasper Marlow's resume encompasses credits as a producer, playwright and screenwriter, across film, theatre and commercials. His first full-length play *Zetland* debuted at the 2010 Sydney Fringe Festival where it was nominated for Best New Work at the Fringe Awards. He has been a member of atyp's Fresh INK ensemble 2009/2010 and received mentorship from Lachlan Philpot, Matthew Whittet and Jane Fitzgerald. An avid theatre writer, his short plays have been performed in Tasmania and New South Wales. These include: *Deep Space 9mm* (Onefest-Hobart, 2009), *Stories from the 428* (Sidetrack Theatre, 2010), *Zetland* (Sidetrack Theatre, 2010) and *ACL* (*Tell It Like It Isn't*, atyp, 2011).Trained at the Australian Film Television and Radio School, his debut short film *Reception* has been an Official Selection in both local and overseas Film Festivals. Most recently it won Best Thriller/ Horror at the Hollywood International Student Film Festival where Jasper was invited to attend the ceremony and received the award from legendary Actor Edward Asner (*Up*, *El-Dorado*). He is currently working on a new play and short film which, fingers crossed, will be completed before the 2012 Armageddon.

## JOANNA ERSKINE (*Boot*)

Joanna Erskine is a graduate of the NIDA Playwright's Studio and a core writer for atyp's Fresh Ink in 2010. Her writing career kick-started after winning the STC Young Playwrights Award for her first play, *Waiting for the 9.07*. She has undertaken residencies with La Mama NYC in Umbria, Playwriting Australia, the Bundanon Trust, Shopfront Theatre and has been a delegate at World Interplay. Plays include *K.I.J.E.* (Old Fitzroy Theatre), *Boot* (*Tell It Like It Isn't*, atyp, 2011), *Bye Bye Baby* (Slide Bar), *Little Mouse* (Brand Spanking New), *Clippings* (NIDA), *Foot* (Griffin Theatre's 24 hour Play Generator), *Baby Doll* (Stories from the 428) and *Midsummer Madness, Macbeth: Undone* (Bell Shakespeare Learning). She is a member of playwright's collective ISM and is currently in development with CRY HAVOC for her play *Rosaline*. She blogs about all things playwriting at www. joannaerskine.com/cluster/

## NAKKIAH LUI (*Brown Lips*)

Nakkiah Lui grew up in Dhurag community in Western Sydney. She believes this is where her passion for writing came from; sharing the contemporary Indigenous experience through performance. Nakkiah was a founding member of the Indigenous Theatre Company 'Nangami'. She then wrote *My Dreaming, Our Awakening*, the first radio play on the ABC Radio National 'Awaye'. Nakkiah was a writer for 'Represent' to create a TV Series based on the lives of youth around Sydney. Nakkiah directed/wrote *From Drag King to Law Queen* (follows an Aboriginal law student's journey to Drag Queen fame) and *BabyGirl*, was shown at the Chauvel cinema , ABC and NITV. Nakkiah is currently completing her Arts/Laws at the University of New South Wales. Nakkiah was a resident in atyp's Fresh Ink Playwright Residency 2010 and a playwright for the show *Tell It Like It Isn't*, atyp, 2011 (*Brown Lips*). Nakkiah is a Playwriting Australia Resident at Belvoir for 2012.

## CHRIS SUMMERS (*Burnt*)

Chris Summers is an Australian playwright. He has won the Sydney Theatre Company Young Playwright's Award, the St. Martin's National Playwriting Award, the Union House Theatre Script Development Award and been short listed for the R.E. Ross Trust Award. His commission from Union House Theatre, *No Place Like*, had a sell-out season in the Guild Theatre, May 2011. His commission from Platform Youth Theatre, *Crossed*, was featured in PlayWriting Australia's National Play Festival 2011 and produced at La Mama Courthouse in June 2011. Works in development include *Rat* (La Mama, March 2012), *Roots* and a mentorship with Arena Theatre Company's Chris Kohn, *Ghost Train*. Chris completed his Bachelor of Creative Arts (Honours) / Bachelor of Law at the University of Melbourne in December 2011 after studies on exchange in Austin, Texas, and will study for a Graduate Diploma in Playwriting at NIDA in 2012.

## SARAH HOPE (*Elissa Louisa Smith Loves William Cornelius Bennett Forever*)

Sarah Hope is an emerging playwright and theatre maker who graduated from the University of Queensland with a Bachelor of Arts majoring in Drama and Film Studies in 2008. During her studies, Sarah undertook a dramaturgical secondment for La Boite Theatre Company. Since graduating, Sarah has gained experience in a variety of theatrical projects as a director, writer, producer and performer in Brisbane and Darwin. She co-wrote and directed *The Keeper* for Tin Can Theatre in 2009. After facilitating a theatre program in Yirrkala in 2009, Sarah moved to Darwin. In 2010 she worked with Arts Access Darwin and CemeNTworx Theatre to devise and direct *Jules Hearts Romeo*, an adaptation of *Romeo and Juliet* for actors with a range of abilities. After attending the Fresh Ink National Studio in 2010 her piece was produced as part of atyp's 2011 season of *Tell It Like It Isn't*. Sarah directed and devised *Sandfly 0820*, a new work for the inaugural Parap Arts Festival in 2011.

## VANESSA BATES (*First Light*)

An award-winning writer, Vanessa Bates' plays include: *Every Second*, *Porn.Cake* (Malthouse Theatre, Griffin Independent), *Checklist for an Armed Robber* (Vitalstatistix, theatre@risk, Belvoir B-Sharp, Deckchair

Theatre), *Match* (Tantrum Theatre) and *Darling Oscar* (Sydney Theatre Company, Black Swan Theatre). Vanessa has written several monologues/solo performance plays including *Hunger* (Griffin), *The World's Tiniest Monkey* (NovemberISM),*The Magic Hour, The Night We Lost Jenny* (New Theatre) and *Homemade* (New Theatre) and is proud to have mentored many writers featured in this book. Vanessa is PWA Playwright in Residence at Griffin Theatre, a graduate of NIDA Playwrights' Studio and one-seventh of playwrights' company 7-ON.

## TIM SPENCER (*Fun in a Cup*)

Tim Spencer is an actor, writer and theatre maker. Whilst studying a Bachelor of Arts/Commerce he performed and directed numerous shows at Sydney University Dramatic Society. In 2010 the performance he created in Shopfront Theatre's ArtsLab *Words They Make with their Mouths* won the People's Choice Award in the Adelaide Fringe Festival. In the same year he wrote and performed in *I Scare My 6 Year Old Self* (Underbelly Arts), *At the Drive In* (Shopfront Theatre) and *The Pursued, The Pursuing, The Busy* and *The Tired* (Brand Spanking New). Since co-founding Bambina Borracha Productions he has produced, written and performed for shows in Sydney, Melbourne and Adelaide including *Beyond the Neck* (B Sharp) and *Under Milk Wood* (Sidetrack Theatre). In 2011 he was mentored by the Belgian theatre company Ontroerend Goed. His monologue *Fun in a Cup* was performed as part of *Tell It Like It Isn't* (atyp, 2011) and his performance *Show Me Yours, I'll Show You Mine* appeared in The Horse's Mouth Festival (Tamarama Rock Surfers). For more information visit his website at www.timspencer.com.au

## JESSICA BELLAMY (*Little Love*)

Jessica Bellamy is a Sydney-based playwright and a Griffin Playwriting Australia Associate Playwright for 2011-12. She holds a Graduate Diploma of Dramatic Art in Playwriting (NIDA) and Bachelor of Arts (Honours) (UNSW). In 2011 she premiered *Sprout* at the Old Fitzroy Theatre (winner of the Rodney Seaborn Playwrights Award, 2011), which will tour to Melbourne in 2012. In 2011 she was commissioned to write *A Fourth of Nature* (a play for 18 young performers) for the ACT Department of Education's School Spectacular, wrote and performed Celebrity Healing for Canberra's You Are Here Festival and Griffin Theatre's Griffringe, had a monologue included in atyp's

*Tell It Like It Isn't* (currently being adapted into a short film, *Bat Eyes*, slated for a February 2012 release) and had an excerpt of *Endless Light and Endless Sound* shown at the PWA National Play Festival. Jessica has tutored playwriting for 'Workshops in the Arts for People with a Disability' through Riverside Theatres, and for atyp. Other work includes *Fast Kill and Bill* (Griffin Theatre Playoffs, 2009/10), and short screenplay *Hirsute* (Melbourne Underground Film Festival, 2010), as well as collaborating on a writer-led Griffringe project, *A Very Crappy Christmas*. Her writing has been staged in *Brand Spanking New* (New Theatre, 2008/09) and *Hot Shorts* (Byron Bay Theatre, 2009).

PHIL SPENCER (*Mike*)

Since graduating in 2007 from the University of Glasgow, Phil Spencer has worked professionally as a writer, director and performer in both the UK and Australia. His Theatre credits include *The Great Apeth* (The Horse's Mouth Festival), *Boxing Day* (Tin Shed, MakeBeLive & TRS, The Old Fitzroy Theatre, Sydney), *Bluey* (Sydney Theatre Company, The Old Fitzroy Theatre, Battersea Arts Centre, London, The Arches, Glasgow), *Mike* (atyp, 2011), *Kansas* (The Home Brew Festival 2010, Sydney), *Yolk* (Brand Spanking New, Sydney), *Fit For A King* (Brand Spanking New and The Arches), *Cardboard Castle* (Imagine Festival, Sydney, The Arches and Edinburgh Fringe Festival), *Shop Lifters of the World* (Carriageworks, Sydney), and *Collisions Can Be Painful* (West End Festival, Glasgow). Phil is co-artistic director of Tin Shed and Associate Artistic Director of Tamarama Rock Surfers Theatre Company.

FINN O'BRANAGÁIN (*Pink Fireworks*)

Finn O'Branagáin has performed and presented work at festivals and events nationally, including the Darwin and Melbourne Fringe Festivals, the National Young Writers' Festival, Wordstorm, and the inaugural Nightwords festival at the Sydney Opera House. She has been a finalist of the NT Young Achiever of the Year Award, and a winner and finalist in the Fist Full of Films Festival. Her co-written work *Dancing Back Home* toured with JUTE and Mudlark theatre. In 2011 she was mentored by Lachlan Philpott as part of the Australia Council's JUMP program through Youth Arts Queensland, and as part of this, showcased her work at Corrugated Iron Youth Arts' TEASE festival, the State Library of Queensland, and at atyp in the Sydney Fringe Festival. Finn was also a 2011 Darwin Theatre Company

Independent Artist, a Backbone Ensemble Member, performing with them at the 2High Festival and collaborating on *The Room v2* for the World Theatre Festival, and also an Express Media National Young Writers' Month Ambassador. In 2012 she will be studying the postgraduate Playwriting course at NIDA.

ZOE HOGAN (*Principal*)

Zoe Hogan is an emerging playwright and former member of atyp's Fresh Ink ensemble. Plays include *Eve* (New Theatre), *Principal* (*Tell It Like It Isn't*, atyp, 2011), *Gosling* (Sydney Theatre Company Young Playwrights Award), *Deaf* (Griffin Theatre Festival of New Writing) and *Small Life*, which was selected for development at Playwriting Australia's National Play Festival in 2011 and Fraser Studios' Off the Shelf program in 2010. Zoe has been a delegate at World Interplay, a staff writer for Inspire Foundation and continues to collect stories from her current home of East Timor.

EMRYS QUIN (*That's What I am Now*)

Emrys Quin is a young playwright twice published with Currency Press as part of the Page to Stage initiative. The reading of his play *In the Company of Dead Cats* during Playwriting Australia's Kicking Down the Doors program lead to his Off the Shelf residency with Queen Street Studio, during which the same play was dramaturged and given a live reading. He has recently undergone his first experience writing and directing a production, *The Future Historians*—staged in August by the UNSW comedy society Studio Four of which Emrys is the 2012 president. When he found out he was part of the National Studio Emrys kissed his local grocer. He now gets significant discounts.

GEORGIA SYMONS (*Twisted*)

Georgia Symons is a writer, director and producer for theatre, film, and radio. She has studied writing in its various forms at NIDA (Young Writers and Directors Studio), Metroscreen (ArtStart Young Screenwriters' Program), UTS, and as a member of this year's atyp Fresh Ink Young Writers' Ensemble. Her first short work for theatre, *Mollycoddled*, was performed in the 2011 Short + Sweet Theatre Festival, Sydney. She was subsequently awarded the Best New Talent Award in the festival. She has had her work published twice in the UTS *Writers' Anthology*. Her short film, *Tell*, was nominated for

Best Experimental Film at the Golden Eye Film Festival. Her theatre directing credits include *Beach* (Timothy Daly, Fort Productions), *Ruby Moon* (Matt Cameron, Hatter Productions), *Margin Walker* (Luke Scholes, Short + Sweet Sydney) and *Dangerous Lenses* (Brooke Robinson, Queen Street Studios residency). Georgia is currently studying Media Arts and Production at UTS

## BROOKE ROBINSON (*Hunger*)

Brooke Robinson has a BA (English) from the University of Sydney and a Graduate Diploma in Creative Writing from UTS where she received the Outstanding Student Award for coming first place. In 2009 she received a $5000 Youth Action Participation Association (YAPA) grant for theatre omnibus project Friends in Danger. In 2010 she had three short plays feature in *Stories from the 428* (Sidetrack Theatre and Sydney Fringe Festival) which will be published in 2012. Recent work includes two developments at Queen Street Studios, *Ebony and...* (Blueprints devised work residency) and *Dangerous Lenses* (Play, Me development program).

## ALICE COOPER (*The Circle of Life*)

Alice Cooper is a performer, writer and theatre-maker based in Sydney. Her current work explores the human relationship to ordinary objects. Her hope is that through performance, she can transform the everyday into sources of wonderment. During her time completing her Bachelor of Creative Arts degree from Melbourne University, Alice wrote, directed and acted in several university productions. In 2007 Alice moved to Paris, where she completed the first year of actor training at L'Ecole Philippe Gaulier. In 2010 Alice was a resident artist at Shopfront Contemporary Arts Centre Sydney in their Artslab program. In the later part of 2010 Alice extended her performance practice by training and performing with the Ensemble at PACT Centre for Emerging Artists. Alice took her solo show *Clown Lights Stage* on a national tour to the Adelaide, Sydney and Melbourne Fringe Festivals in 2011. In May 2011 she performed as Silvius in Siren Theatre's *As You Like It* at Carriageworks. Alice is currently undertaking a Fresh Ink mentorship with Australian Theatre for Young People where she is mentored by Rosie Dennis. She tweets regularly about theatre and other interests at @alicemarycooper and blogs about her practice at alicemarycooper.com.

## SARAH GAUL (*The Last Post*)

When her parents took Sarah Gaul to see *The Sound of Music* at age 9, Sarah's life was never the same again. She threw herself in school and community theatre, later progressing to opera and operetta. After High School, Sarah joined Tantrum Theatre's Emerging Writers Program, eventuating in the production of Sarah's one-act play, *Three Days*, mentored through the process by Ross Mueller. In 2010, Sarah worked as an intern for Ross, as well as Debra Oswald, as part of Playwriting Australia's National Playwriting Festival. After failing to get into acting school for two years, Sarah commenced a Law degree at ANU, Canberra, in 2010. She wrote and performed in the Arts Revue, and had the lead in *Kiss Me Kate*, so it wasn't all bad. She auditioned again for acting schools and much to her relief was accepted into VCA, studying Drama, in 2011. She loves living in Melbourne, and spending all her cash on strong coffee and theatre tickets.

## ALEXANDRA MACALISTER-BILLS (*La Conversación*)

Alexandra Macalister- Bills grew up jumping waves and reading fairytales in Far East Gippsland before moving to Melbourne to study. Alexandra graduated from the University of Melbourne in 2011 where she completed a Bachelor of Arts with a double major in Creative Writing and Cultural Studies, as well as a concurrent Diploma in Spanish. She is addicted to travelling and has let herself get lost in South-East Asia and South America. Her travels have taught her to never underestimate the impact of the everyday, which she hopes is reflected in her writing. Alexandra also dabbles in short fiction, poetry, travel writing and text based art although she has a tendency to ignore these boundaries and cross-pollinate.

## CAROLYN BURNS (*Stick*)

Carolyn Burns graduated from the University of Edinburgh with a Master's in Literature and Modernity in 2009. She also holds a Bachelor of Commerce and a Bachelor of Arts (Honours) from the University of Sydney, where she is currently a PhD candidate in the Department of English, conducting research into adaptation and twentieth century lyric drama. While at the University of Sydney, Carolyn has been extensively involved in student publications, writing regularly for *Honi Soit* and *The Bull*, and served as an editor of *Hermes*, the University of Sydney Union's annual literary anthology. Carolyn's first two plays, *Careers for Attractive Ladies* (2010) and *Mongrel* (2011) were both official selections of the Sydney Fringe Festival. She is currently developing a situation comedy about a high school debating team.

## ALEX CULLEN (*Senseless*)

Alex Cullen has written for theatre and television. She is a graduate of the NIDA Playwrights Studio, 2007, and has a Bachelor of Creative Arts from Wollongong University. She has studied at AFTRS, and attended World Interplay. Alex was part of Playwriting Australia's Graduate Studio, National Script Workshop 2008. Her plays include *Snapped* (The Old Fitzroy Theatre), *The Devil has a Townhouse in Tamworth* (New Theatre, Leftovers, Parade Studio), and *Trolley Boys* (Old Fitzroy Theatre, Metro Arts). She worked as a sketch writer for Comedy Channel's *Off their Rockers*. Alex is currently an Associate Artist in Residence at Playwriting Australia and is a playwright in atyp's Fresh Ink program.

## ALYSHA HERRMANN (*Ben Thomas, I Love You*)

Alysha Herrmann is a proud parent and regional artist working across disciplines in the arts, community development and education to develop work, which respects and enriches both the audience and her creative collaborators. Alysha is also currently completing a Teaching/Arts degree externally and was the 2011 South Australian Young Citizen of the Year. Along the road Alysha has been a high school dropout, teenage mum, single parent, waitress, artist, student, sewing machinist, blogger, dishwasher, community facilitator, speaker and many other things in between. Alysha believes in the role of arts and cultural activities in building community morale and inspiration and is committed to social justice outcomes in everything she does as a parent, employee, volunteer and passionate community member. As an artist, Alysha is a playwright, poet, director, performer and facilitator and was an inaugural Australia Council JUMP Mentee in 2010. For information on past and current projects visit http://alyshaherrmann.wordpress.com

## LAURA HOPKINSON (*Prince Willy*)

Laura Hopkinson is a Sydney-based writer, performer, director, moss collector and aspiring puppeteer. Her short works have been featured in short festivals at Griffin and MKA. *Bumblebee*, a play which she co-wrote and directed, was awarded best play at the 2009 Fast and Fresh Festival, bringing the play to Short and Sweet the following year. Laura has also written for Griffin Theatre Company's 24 hour Junior Play-offs. In 2010 she was selected for Sydney Theatre Company's Young Playwrights' Residency and was awarded a mentorship at Playwrighting Australia as a co-winner of the Kicking Down The Door competition. She also finished her HSC. Laura has been a Literary Intern at Griffin Theatre Company and a member of youth advisory teams at Sydney Theatre Company, atyp, Griffin Theatre Company and the Sydney Opera House.

# www.currency.com.au

Visit Currency Press' website now to:

- Buy your books online
- Browse through our full list of titles, from plays to screenplays, books on theatre, film and music, and more
- Choose a play for your school or amateur performance group by cast size and gender
- Obtain information about performance rights
- Find out about theatre productions and other performing arts news across Australia
- For students, read our study guides
- For teachers, access syllabus and other relevant information
- Sign up for our email newsletter

**The performing arts publisher**